TAKE CONTROL
of Your
Subconscious Mind

Andy,
Nice to meet you!
Tony Balle

TAKE CONTROL

of Your
Subconscious Mind

A Practical Approach
to Creating Focus and
Becoming More Successful

Anthony T. Galie

Cornerstone Press ■ Florida

Cornerstone Press
2145 North Highway A1A
Indialantic, FL 32903

e-mail: goals4u@msn.com
(321) 777-1718 ■ fax (321) 777-8995

Book design & copy editing by Sara Patton
Printed in the USA

ISBN #0-9671310-0-6
Library of Congress #00-090541

Contents

*To Adam Michael Galie, my father,
the finest and most honest man
I have ever met.*

Acknowledgments

There are many people I would like to thank for help with this book.

First and most important, my wife Catherine was an ever-present source of inspiration and help in constructing this project. I simply could not have done it without her.

Dr. Jack Ryalls generously devoted his time to offering editing suggestions and I am sincerely grateful.

Mr. Bill Cates was remarkably supportive and saved me an enormous amount of time with his publishing expertise.

Ms. Sara Patton, the best editor I have ever met, was patient and thorough in her editorial suggestions.

Marc and Jon Reede, whose invaluable marketing expertise has helped me to reach my own goals.

Finally, Mr. Bob Davies, from Human Performance Training, guided me every step of the way.

Preface

What is consciousness? Since this book deals almost exclusively with the subconscious mind and how to program it, it is appropriate to begin with a discussion on what it means to be conscious. When asked, most people will tell you that consciousness equals awareness. But that is not the case. There is a simple way to disprove this notion. Do you fall out of bed at night while sleeping? Most people do not fall out of bed, yet they also do not lie still. If you have ever seen time-lapse photography of sleeping individuals, it is apparent that they roam all over the boundaries of the bed and yet they do not fall out. Why is this so? Because even though a person is completely unconscious—they are asleep—they are still very aware of the boundaries of the bed.

Many people define consciousness as thinking, yet this is also not the case. Have you ever tried to solve a problem and simply could not come up with a solution? So you leave it and begin doing something else. Then, hours later when you are consciously engaged in a completely different activity, the solution to your problem pops into your mind fully developed. The thinking that took place to solve the problem was a completely *subconscious* process.

Your consciousness is not even a continuous process. You feel as though you are continually aware of your surroundings, but in fact people tend to drift in and out of consciousness thousands of times a day. Try to remember the last time you drove to work. If that drive took you 20 minutes, how many of those 20 minutes were you fully conscious of driving? You will be lucky if you can accurately recall two to three minutes of the time, because most people spend the majority of their lives thinking about what they should have done, could have done, or hope to do, and paying very little attention to what they actually *are* doing.

In order to understand what consciousness is, you need to understand a little about how the nervous system works. Nerves are never found in isolation. They are always connected to other nerve cells, and these cells are grouped together into systems which are always connected to other systems. These systems exhibit the quality of "mutual inhibition." As one nervous system activates, it tends to depress or inhibit the system that is connected to it.

For example, going to sleep looks as if you are turning something off. Previously the person was active and mobile and now he or she is unconscious. Actually, going to sleep is very much a process of turning something *on.* Put simply, human beings have an activation system and a depression system. While you are awake and alert, the system that allows you to sleep is being inhibited. And once you fall asleep, the system that allows you to be active and mobile is being depressed.

The more complex the nervous system, the more inhibition is typically present. For example, if you chop off the head of a chicken, what does it do? It runs around like a chicken without a head. The headless chicken does not immediately fall over and stop moving. When you isolate the brain from the rest of the body, all of the muscles begin to fire simultaneously. The main function of the brain is to control and inhibit all of the different systems. If you have ever seen a person experiencing a *grand mal* epileptic seizure, you have observed what happens when the brain stops inhibiting muscle movements. Without the brain to inhibit them, every muscle fires simultaneously and uncontrollably.

If you decided right now to reach down with your right hand and pick up a pencil, that would be a very *conscious* movement. It would also be a very *inhibited* movement. In order to pick up the pencil, your brain would have to keep dozens of muscles under control and fire the nerve cells in certain motor systems while inhibiting the activation of others, all in a tightly controlled sequence. The more complicated the movement, the more inhibition is involved.

Look at the X below. What do you see? Take another look and ask yourself again, what do you see?

Chances are you saw only the X. When you looked at it, you were very *conscious* of the letter and thus you inhibited everything else, but in fact what your eyes saw was the letter X as well as the printed words above it and below it. You probably also saw your hands holding the book. And you may have even seen what the book was resting on. All of this visual information was sent to your brain, but because your attention was directed to the letter X, you inhibited everything else. To a significant degree then, consciousness equals inhibition, and the more conscious you are of something, the more inhibited you become.

If I told you that you could double your income next year, you might respond by saying that was impossible. You might tell me that you are not experienced enough, or that your territory is saturated, or that no one in your field has ever doubled their income in a single year's time. Explain what people can do, and they almost always focus on what cannot be done. Consciousness has made them inhibited. If I asked you to tell me a funny joke, you might reply that you are not good at relating stories. Yet, if you were hypnotized and I suggested to your subconscious mind that you would tell a joke, you would do so without hesitation and without inhibition.

Intoxicated people sometimes say and do things they would never do while sober because alcohol chemically disinhibits them. The beauty of the subconscious mind is that it is able to tap into this simpler way of thinking. You cannot force the subconscious mind to do anything. What you *can* do is systematically set the conditions to bring about the desired response. For example, you cannot make yourself go to sleep at night. If you have ever been awake at night trying to get to sleep—and who has never experienced sleeplessness?—you have experienced the futility of trying to force your subconscious mind to act. Usually you fall asleep the moment you stop trying. You cannot make yourself go to sleep, but you can set certain conditions that signal to the unconscious mind what you want it to do. Some people lie in a certain position, or count sheep, or place themselves mentally in a particular frame of mind and then can fall asleep within a few minutes. By deliberately setting the conditions, the door to the unconscious is opened.

Throughout this book you will be shown a series of hands-on techniques that will allow you to internalize your goals quickly and easily by setting the proper conditions for obtaining a successful outcome. Once you learn the rules by which your subconscious mind operates, you can free yourself from the inhibiting thoughts of the conscious mind and release your potential from within.

Introduction

Near my home on the coast of central Florida is one of the world's largest nesting areas for the loggerhead and leatherback sea turtles. These magnificent creatures have existed since prehistoric times, and over millions of years they have evolved some very complicated mating and reproductive behaviors. During the summer months when the moon is full, female turtles travel back to lay their eggs on the exact beach where they were born.

On many occasions, I've had the opportunity to witness this ritual. In the middle of the night the turtle drags itself up onto the beach and, using its flippers, digs a large hole to lay its eggs. After digging the hole and laying its eggs, it buries the nest and then crawls back into the sea. Once this ritual has begun, the turtle literally cannot stop itself. It is an instinctive behavior. If the turtle were picked up and taken a mile down the beach, it would crawl back to the exact spot it was taken from, pick up where it left off, and continue until the egg-laying ritual was complete. This animal will not let any outside noise or distraction to allow it to deviate from its preprogrammed course of action.

At the time that these behaviors evolved, they were extremely beneficial to the animal's survival. In fact, for thousands of years this system worked just fine. The problem is that the world has changed and the turtle has not. As the beaches have become more developed, the fragile nests are frequently disturbed and the eggs often destroyed. Street and home lights have disoriented the animal, sometimes causing it to lay its eggs too far from the water, and unless it changes its behavior this ancient reptile is very likely to become extinct. This inability to adapt to a rapidly changing world threatens its very existence.

Many businesspeople share similarities with the sea turtle. In a world where the economic and business climate changes almost overnight, it will be those individuals who can quickly modify and reprogram their behaviors who will persevere and become the true success stories of the future. Unfortunately, change is something that most of us did not learn how to do in school. Most people have not taken a "Goal-setting 101" course in college.

The book you are reading is designed to show you a series of simple, hands-on techniques that can be used to effect real change in your life. Congratulations. You've made the first step down that path.

1

Change Your Life in 21 Days

I am in a very interesting position. For nearly 20 years, I have been traveling throughout the country teaching a program called "The Subconscious Aspects of Business." It is a goal-setting program that revolves around some simple concepts. First, correctly or incorrectly, I assume that participants have some goals they would like to achieve. These goals may be related to their business or their personal lives. Many who attend my seminars have even taken the time to write their goals down on a piece of paper, and if you have done that, I congratulate you. That is an important step. The fact is, most people have no goals or direction whatsoever. Most people spend more time planning their vacation every year than they do planning their lives. I call them "unguided missiles." They sound dangerous, don't they?

To illustrate my point, try this simple experiment. In the next 24 hours ask at least ten people, "Where do you see yourself five years from today?" Then observe their responses. On average, nine out of ten people will give you a "deer-caught-in-the-headlights look," break eye contact with you, and then stare up to the ceiling while they try to find an answer. Many will bring their hand up to their face, in what is known as the "evaluation gesture." After approximately 10 to 15 seconds, they will look at you again and give you a vague answer such as, "I want to be making more money" or "Doing a lot better in my job."

Some people make New Year's resolutions or do complete quarterly or annual reviews of their business performance. Often there is little difficulty identifying the targets, but the real question should be: Once you have set these goals, what are you doing to stay focused on them and motivated toward achieving them? Most people who have been in business for more than just a few weeks rapidly discover that

> **People who really have their "act together" have learned how to program certain habits into their mind.**

the motivation to achieve one's goals has a nasty habit of disappearing. It simply does not last very long. We listen to a good motivational speaker or attend an inspiring conference and we feel great. We are pumped up, inspired, and motivated, and the way to achieve our goals seems so clear, vivid, and attainable at that moment. But how long does that feeling last? Most people are already beginning to lose their drive as they leave the conference. And for those who are a little more motivated, the longest that feeling typically lasts is 48 hours.

A week later these people have drifted back to their old level of performance. Yet, every once in a while you encounter someone who really has their "act together": someone who is highly driven and seems to be in a good mood all of the time. They know where they are going and how they are going to get there. This does not happen by accident. More often than not, these individuals have learned how to tap into the power of their subconscious mind, and they systematically set the conditions to bring forth this desired response. They have learned how to program certain successful habits into their mind.

Successful people program themselves.

Fortunately, it does not take long to develop a new habit. Typically a new habit can be programmed into your subconscious mind within 21 days. For example, let's say that your goal is to go out and meet one new business contact every day. If you could discipline yourself to find the time to do that for 21 days in a row, within a month you would develop the habit of generating new contacts daily. You would rearrange yourself mentally and subconsciously. It would become second nature to you. As you were getting up for work in the morning one of the first thoughts to pop into your mind might be: "I have a really busy day today. It's filled with meetings. When am I going to find the time to pick up the phone and go out and generate some of those potential contacts?"

By learning to stay focused for a month, you will develop a new successful habit and do it unconsciously. The good news is that it does not take a very long time to do all of this. It really can be that simple—doing something for 21 days in a row internalizes the goal. What you will learn in the following chapters is exactly how to set these conditions for success.

As you perform the simple focusing techniques outlined in this book, in 21 days you can literally set your mind on achieving your goals. You will be able to program your subconscious to make the behaviors that are important to achieving your goals habitual in nature.

This book will help you program your mind to perform functions on a consistent basis that will make you a more successful professional. The most important points to keep in mind are:

1.   It takes approximately 21 days to form a new habit. It does not take 21 years, or even 21 weeks, to change a person's behavior. It can usually be accomplished in one month or less, provided it is done consistently. Do anything over and over again 21 days in a row and it is likely to turn into an unconscious, habitual behavior.

2.   You can teach your subconscious to focus on these new habits by training your mind through simple exercises involving rewards and punishment, visualization, and passive listening techniques. These concepts might sound complicated at first, but they are actually quite simple.

3.   While some systems may teach you tricks for getting ahead, many do not deal with the root of what holds us back: waning motivation. Even though it takes only 21 days to form a new habit, the motivation and drive required to develop such a habit usually only last a couple of days. This is why most people don't stay on their diets (losing weight over a couple of weeks is very rewarding, but the cake is more immediately gratifying). And it is why most salespeople don't set appointments habitually

(the rewards of setting appointments every day would produce a huge yearly income, but the fear of rejection today is immediate). This book addresses the issue of motivation and shows you how you can stick with your program.

Let's get started!

2

Program Yourself
for Success

As a motivational speaker, I am often asked to give a key-note address at conventions and sales conferences. In the process I meet some very interesting people. Frequently, I am able to observe who gets called up on stage to win the awards: "Agent of the Year," "Top Money-Maker," "Number 1 Producer," "The Quality Award Winner," etc. Some years ago I developed a habit that has served me well. When I see these top achievers winning their awards, I make it a point to introduce myself to them, congratulate them on their achievement, and then ask a very simple question: "What do you do to get and stay motivated?"

When I first started doing this, I was pleasantly surprised to find that nearly all of the top achievers were able to answer this question. When queried, every single one of them could pinpoint exactly what they do to stay focused and prevent them from losing their drive. Often they would say something like, "That is an interesting question. No one has ever asked me that before. But since you ask, *this* is what I do to stay motivated."

The point is that they are all doing something. They are all on a "program" for success. You are not likely to wake up one morning and spontaneously develop motivation. It is a state that needs to be developed over time in an organized way. My research has shown that top achievers systematically do certain things to keep themselves fired up, focused, and energized. And these behaviors are usually done on a daily basis.

Successful people are not all doing exactly the same thing, however. Not by any stretch of the imagination. There is room for individual differences. I have interviewed hundreds of top performers in dozens of different professions, and I do not believe that there is a single, universal way to program yourself for success. There are, in fact, hundreds — if not thousands — of ways it can be accomplished.

For example, not too long ago, I spoke in Los Angeles to a large real estate group where I met a young man who had made over $4 million in commissions that year selling high-priced homes in Beverly Hills. I asked what he did to stay focused and, without blinking an eye, he fired back: "I write my goals down three times a week." He explained that he found out early on in his career that if he could not see the goals written down, if they were not in front of him on a piece of paper, he would lose his focus and become disorganized. So he began to keep a yellow legal pad in the upper right-hand corner of his desk, and two or three times a week he would take a few moments and rewrite his business objectives. He had very clear-cut daily, quarterly, and yearly production goals. By writing them down, he was able to visualize them, focus on them, and stay motivated.

Most people would quickly see benefits if they took five minutes, three times a week, to write their goals on a piece of paper.

Writing your goals down three times a week is an excellent example of what I mean by systematic self-programming. This successful real estate agent's act of repeatedly transferring his goals onto paper continually remotivated him and helped him remain focused long enough to actually reach his desired objectives.

In all likelihood, this is not the first time you have heard of the benefit of writing your goals down continuously. It is a common approach to basic goal-setting. The problem is that most people simply refuse to do it. Some people have told me that writing their goals down over and over again was "very boring." Others explain that, with their busy schedules, they cannot find the time. It is a great idea, but in terms of practical application, it is simply not something that many people will actually do. Yet most people would quickly and dramatically see benefits if they actually took five minutes, three times a week, to write their goals on a piece of paper.

Here is another excellent example of programming the subconscious mind. Not long ago, I met a woman who was the vice president of a large insurance company. When I asked what she did to keep herself motivated, she said that every day on the way into the office she spends 10 or 15 minutes listening to motivational tapes. She used to listen to radio talk shows on the way into work, but she discovered that they depressed her. So a number of years ago she began keeping about half a dozen sales and motivational tapes in her glove compartment. It was easy to reach over and pop one of the tapes into her tape player every morning. By the time she arrived at the office, she was in a good mood, thinking positive thoughts in the back of her mind, and often had a better day because of her enthusiasm.

One time, in the middle of one of my presentations, an older gentlemen stopped me and commented, "Son, it is the Bible. Everything that you talk about in your seminars, such as goal-setting, motivation, and positive thinking, is all to be found somewhere in the Good Book." He told me that his program for success was to read the Bible for a half hour every night before he went to sleep. He stated that for years this simple nightly ritual had kept him motivated, inspired, and "on the straight and narrow." I believe this is also an excellent example of programming yourself for success.

> **Successful people motivate themselves every day.**

There are probably hundreds of individual ways by which you can program yourself to achieve your goals. But if you categorize the techniques, there are three main pathways into the subconscious mind. They are:

- Visually
- Auditorially, and
- Kinesthetically.

These words sound technical, but the concepts behind them are very basic. This book presents a series of simple, hands-on techniques using these pathways that will enable you, over a reasonable period of time, to become focused on your personal and business goals and remain that way.

This presupposes that you already have some goals you would like to achieve. So, before we go any further, let's take a moment to clearly identify some objectives. We'll do this together in the next chapter.

3

Set Your Goals

Research has shown that the act of writing things down helps cement them in our subconscious. So writing down business and personal goals is an excellent way to program them into your subconscious.

Here is one way to do it. Take a piece of paper. Divide it into three sections. Label the column on the far left *Long-Term Goals,* the one in the middle *Mid-Range Goals,* and the right-hand column *Daily Goals.* This table is going to be the foundation for committing your goals to paper and programming them into your mind.

LONG-TERM GOALS (3 to 5 years)	MID-RANGE GOALS (next 30 to 90 days)	DAILY GOALS

By my definition, a long-term goal is a target or an objective that typically takes between three to five years to accomplish. Of course, your particular goals may be achieved sooner or may take longer than that. But for now, let's think about a three- to five-year time frame. Where do you see yourself five years from today? Where do you want to be working? How much money would you like to be making? What kind of house would you like to be living in? These are examples of long-term goals.

You have probably already noticed that the emphasis here is on material objectives. It is entirely possible that your goals are more personal or esoteric in nature. Often people say something like, "Within five years, I want to have traveled around the world," or "I would like to be a deacon in my church," or "My dream is to run in the Boston marathon," or perhaps "I hope to be involved in a successful relationship." It is not really important that your individual goals be material in nature. What *is* important is that you have "a dream," a vision that you are working toward.

There is a frequently encountered statement in my business that is really quite true: "If you don't have dreams, chances are you will have nightmares." You should also note that the long-term dream does not necessarily need to be all that "realistic." Here is why. Assume you have two salespeople of exactly equal ability. The first person is dreaming about making $500,000 within five years, while the second person dreams of making $250,000 within five years. Which of those two salespeople is most likely to be making at least $250,000 within five years? The first salesperson, by visualizing that $500,000, is more likely to achieve a higher income level than the salesperson who only aspires to $250,000.

Of course, we cannot predict the future. Just look back at the last five years of your life and ask yourself how much of what happened could have been predicted. While we can't predict the future (perhaps the $250,000-a-year salesperson will win the lottery, as unlikely as that is), by dreaming big you are steering your unconscious mind in the direction that will most *likely* result in future success.

> **If you don't have dreams, chances are you will have nightmares.**

Take a few moments now and write down on a piece of paper a few of the long-term goals that you would like to see yourself achieve within the next three to five years. Begin each sentence with: "I am achieving..."

Next, let's work our way backwards and think in terms of a primary goal for the next year. If you are really going to achieve your five-year plan, what major accomplishment must you achieve this year? Obviously, if you are an upwardly mobile person, you have more than one thing you hope to accomplish in a year's time. However, for the purposes of this exercise, try to pick one clear and vivid objective on which to center your attention. Write it down under the heading of *Long-Term Goals*. If at all possible, this goal should be quantifiable — that is, something you can actually measure. Writing something like "I want to be a better person" is typically too vague for your unconscious mind to respond to. Instead, try something more concrete, such as "I am providing five new services to the community in which I live."

Next, think of a mid-range goal for the next 30 to 90 days. The objective is not to think of the most dramatic scenario or the overall grand plan, but a target to focus upon in the short term. For example, if your goal is to make $100,000 in income this year, your goal for the next 90 days might be to produce $25,000. Write your mid-range goal down under the heading of *Mid-Range Goals*.

A lot of offices have monthly and quarterly goals for their personnel, so coordinating your personal business goals to coincide with your company's schedule is a good idea. Tie your mid-range goal to your daily goal. If your daily goal is to make four appointments a day, your monthly goal could be 80 appointments a month. Review your records to see how many appointments you made last month, the month before, last November — see what numbers you hit and how much you made in income. Maybe you had 20 appointments one month, 40 another. With a monthly goal of 80, your income could be double or quadruple what it was those months. You can see how sticking to a daily, monthly, and yearly goal can mean a real difference to your bottom line.

Be sure to identify a clear-cut deadline for accomplishing your mid-range goal. And — very important — write down the specific activities you will need to perform if you really are going to achieve that goal. What exactly do you need to accomplish to get there? Write down what time you are going to allot to making calls — such as mornings from 8 to 11. How many calls will be new referrals,

> **Write down the specific activities you will need to perform to achieve each goal.**

and how many will be follow-ups on current clients? Write down these activities in full sentences, and have one for each day of the mid-range schedule.

If you do this completely, by the time you are finished you will have, for a monthly schedule, 30 properly written affirmations ready to transcribe onto a goal tape. I will talk more later about how you can use these daily affirmations to remain focused on your goals on a daily basis, just by playing an audio tape of you reading these affirmations out loud. You don't even need to concentrate on listening—just having the tape playing in the background (on your car stereo, in your home, or in your office) will do the trick.

Finally, select a daily goal that you wish to internalize. This is the one behavior that, should you accomplish it each day, would virtually guarantee that you would reach your goals by the end of the year. This objective is really the engine that will ultimately drive you to your long-term goals. A daily goal is something that you are trying to accomplish each and every day. It is the one thing that you get done above all others. It is a classic example of a "good business habit."

Your daily goal should be one you think is realistic for you to meet every day. Perhaps it is a minimum number of calls, or a set number of appointments every day. Don't write down 20 appointments if you know that only three or four is a realistic goal. You don't want to get discouraged by selecting goals that you will not be able to reach. Of course, as you achieve more and more success, you can change your goals to reflect your new aspirations.

Let me give you some actual examples. Not long ago I met a young man from Albany, New York, who sells insurance for one of the largest insurance companies in the country. The year that I met him, he had produced nearly $3 million in premiums, which is a phenomenal amount. I asked him what his daily goal was and, without hesitation, he said that he needed to see five people face-to-face every day. He kept very careful records and knew exactly what his closing ratio was, and his numbers clearly told him that five people face-to-face each day would statistically guarantee that he would reach his year-end goal.

A successful computer salesperson told me that her daily goal was to produce three good, qualified referrals for each appointment that she went to. She said that as far as she was concerned, it almost didn't matter whether she made a sale or not this way, because if she kept producing good referrals she knew the sales would take care of themselves.

If you are trying to lose weight, your daily goal might be to stick to a 1,500-calorie-a-day regimen. Or it might be to get through the day without snacking between meals, or to start your day with a half hour of physical exercise.

So take a moment and ask yourself, "What is the one daily activity that I could be accomplishing that would drive me toward my mid-range and yearly goals?" Write it down on a piece of paper. Take the paper and display it prominently somewhere in your home or office. Unlike long-term goals, daily goals should be very realistic. If you set your daily goal too high, you could be setting yourself up for failure.

Daily goals should be realistic.

Now you have a working outline. As you gain a better understanding of exactly how to program your unconscious mind, you may decide to increase, decrease, change, or even delete some of the goals you have written down. However, you now have a starting point to focus on.

4

Three Pathways Into the Subconscious

There are three primary ways to internalize goals into the subconscious mind: the visual, auditory, and kinesthetic approach.

The Visual Approach

If you listen to top-producing businesspeople, they very often use similar terminologies. It is not uncommon to hear them say something like, "I started ten years ago with no money and little education, and today I am worth millions," or "When I started, I didn't have much going for me, but what I did have was a dream, a vision." They talk about how they would go to bed at night and picture in their mind what kind of car they wanted to drive someday, what kind of house they wanted to live in, and how much money they wanted to earn. And this was not something they did once or twice. They did it often. If you listen, they will tell you that *every* night they would dream about reaching their goals.

One successful builder told me that he and his spouse would "fantasize" about what kind of house they were going to live in once they became financially successful.

They used to drive around affluent neighborhoods in their spare time and then go home and pretend they were designing their dream home. Today, they are living in a mansion which they designed.

Olympic athletes are very big on the power of visualization. When watching the Olympics, you may have noticed that many athletes close their eyes and rehearse their routines in their mind before they go out and attempt to compete. In our culture, we call very successful people "visionaries," and it is for a reason.

Nearly all high achievers are practicing some form of visualization.

Having spent years interviewing high achievers, I have come to the conclusion that nearly all of them are practicing some form of visualization. They are, if you will, "hypnotizing" themselves to reach their goals. Don't let that word scare you. In fact, the average person spends far more time during the day in a hypnotic state than out of one. Have you ever driven past your exit on a freeway, or pulled into your driveway at the end of the day and seriously had to ask yourself, "How did I get here?" "Was that light red?" "Did I stop at that stop sign?" Have you ever seen a member of your family so entranced in front of the television set that you call them for dinner and they don't even hear you call their name? Have you ever experienced a daydream? Stared out into space with a faraway look, not really seeing what you were looking at or hearing what was going on around you? If you've had any of these experiences, then you've experienced hypnosis. This state of mind is certainly nothing to be afraid of. In fact, most top achievers have learned how to deliberately tap into a hypnotic state to program their own subconscious mind.

Once you understand the process of how visualization works, you can learn a simple, five-minute-a-day technique to make visualization work for you. In Chapter 8 you will do just that!

The Auditory Approach

Another pathway into the subconscious mind is the auditory approach. As you hear messages repeatedly playing in the background, many of those messages are picked up subconsciously whether you want them to be or not. You can walk up to nearly anyone and start rattling off a few phrases associated with a common television commercial and, without hesitation, they will usually complete the expression. See if you can fill in the blanks:

- "Winston tastes good ..."
- "Please don't squeeze the ..."
- "You're in good hands with ..."
- "Fly the friendly skies of ..."

The average American knows more than 200 television commercial slogans at the subconscious level. Did you try to learn those commercials? Did you sit down in front of the television set one day and say, "Today I am going to learn the Charmin jingle?" Did you *want* to learn them? Do you think you will ever be able to forget them? Those commercial messages are imbedded very deeply in your mind, and they got there simply by virtue of the fact that they were droning in the background while you were concentrating on other things. Advertisers spend billions of dollars a year on those particular messages because they know that the more familiar you are with a message, the more likely you are to act in a certain way.

Not surprisingly, if you could internalize your goals in the same manner, you would be more likely to increase your activity toward achieving them. In Chapter 10, you will learn exactly how to create a ten-minute-long, personalized goal tape that will allow you to internalize your goals using the auditory approach. At the end of this process, you will have your goals on tape in a very personalized way.

Now comes the easy part. One of the advantages to this process is that you don't even have to listen to the tape. You do not have to pull your car off to the side of the road and pay close attention to what is being said. You were not paying attention to all of those radio and television commercials playing in the background, and yet they are buried in your subconscious mind. The same is true here. When my youngest son, Nicholas, was about two years old, he began watching the Barney program. Every night at 6 p.m. we would turn the program on for him to enjoy. Personally, I didn't care for the program and I certainly was not paying attention to it. But years later I still know many of the songs by heart. Just by being in the same room while those songs were repeatedly playing in the background, I internalized them.

The same can be true for you. If you simply have the tape playing in the background every day for the next 21 days, your subconscious mind will pick up the messages on the tape, passively, with little or no effort on your part.

If you do not like listening to tapes in your car or if you do not have a tape player, you can have the tape playing in the background while you are doing paperwork in the office, while working out, gardening, walking, or virtually any activity at all. As your subconscious repeatedly hears your affirmations, it will become more and more focused on the message, and thus more likely to produce the activity needed to get you there.

The Kinesthetic Approach

Still another pathway into your subconscious mind is the kinesthetic approach. Don't let the word scare you. It simply means using sensations and feelings to sensitize your mind. It is predicated on one of the simplest concepts in psychology: the Pavlovian Theory. The theory is that any event followed by a pleasurable experience is likely to be repeated, whereas any event followed by a punishment will tend to be avoided. This helps explain why a rat tempted by a treat will run through a maze, and why a dog, when offered a biscuit, will roll over on command. And, believe it or not, Pavlov's theory may have a lot to do with why you are currently having success or difficulty reaching your goals.

We are all creatures of habit. A friend of mine once said that in business there are essentially two kinds of habits: good habits and bad habits. There is very little in between. And, as was mentioned earlier, one of the key

Most successful businesspeople have taken the time to program in good business habits.

characteristics of successful businesspeople is that they have taken the time to program in some good business habits. Often these habits are not complicated or even that challenging. My experience has revealed that most top achievers are not working from complicated sales systems or with fancy computer programs. They break down what needs to be done into some very basic daily goals, they discipline themselves to program those goals into their subconscious mind, and then they begin cranking out the numbers.

■　■　■

Of all the different concepts that will be discussed in this book, consistently setting and achieving your daily goals is the single most important thing you can do to become successful. So let's begin by looking at the rules that govern successful people.

Throughout college and graduate school my training was in psychology. Specifically, I was trained to be an experimental psychologist. These are the folks who design experiments to test various psychological theories. One of the crucial parts of any experiment is the statistical analysis of the results. Statistics is at the heart of all of psychology. My problem was that, even though I had a love for psychology, I was never very good at statistics. Throughout my undergraduate years, I was able to get adequate grades by memorizing formulas and spitting them out at test time, but the fact remained that I never truly understood the formulas or the concepts behind them.

When I was admitted to a graduate program, the first and most important course I had to take was Advanced

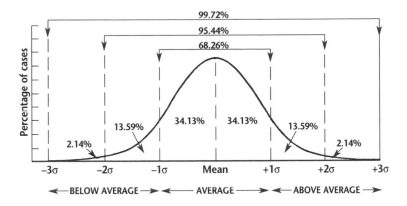

Percentage distribution of cases in a normal curve.

Statistics. Recognizing my weakness in that area, I went to the professor who was to be my instructor. I explained to him my problem and asked for some guidance. Without hesitation, he walked up to the blackboard and drew a bell curve and asked if I knew what it was. I replied that of course I did. Then he asked if I knew what it *meant*. He explained that the bell curve is the basis of all modern statistics. In fact, every single statistical concept in one way, shape, or form is derived from that simple curve. In other words, no bell curve, no statistics. Then he explained how you get a bell curve. By the time he finished describing how the curve affected real-world events, I had a new perspective on statistics. With this new viewpoint I was able to earn an "A" in the course and go on to eventually teach a statistics course! Here is what he explained to me.

A bell curve is derived from a tendency that people (represented in statistics by numbers) have to mostly end up in the middle of the pack. This is known in statistics as the "central limit tendency." Any time you take a large number of purely random events and begin to measure them, these random events begin to organize themselves in the shape of a bell curve. No one knows why this occurs, but it happens every time. If you take a large number of random events and begin to plot where they land on a continuum from infinitely high to infinitely low, inevitably a bell curve shape emerges. You find a small percentage of those events, only about 2 percent, at the very high end of the curve, and 10 to 15 percent fall above the average. Another small percentage of about 2 percent will fall at the very low end of the curve, with 10 to 15 percent falling in the area designated as below average. But the vast majority, about 68 percent, will average out and fall near the middle of the curve.

> **Any time you take a large number of purely random events and begin to measure them, these random events begin to organize themselves in the shape of a bell curve.**

Here is what all that means in plain English. Let's look at some large number of random events and see what the curve predicts. How about something as simple as a New Year's resolution. By far the most common New Year's resolution in America is to lose weight. Let's say you have a million people who on January 1 make a New Year's resolution to lose ten pounds. That, of course, is a large number of random events. The bell curve predicts that if you come back a year later and look at what percentage of those people actually lost the weight and kept it off (in other words, had a "very positive outcome"), you would find that only about 2 percent still had the weight off. The curve also predicts that there would be a percentage of people who actually gained ten pounds and kept it on (a "very negative outcome"). You guessed it—2 percent would do that. But the vast majority—about 68 percent—would have an "average outcome": they would lose a few pounds and eventually gain them back. This is a classic example of the central limit tendency.

Here is another example. If you look at income distribution in America, it typically follows the bell curve almost exactly. There is a percentage of Americans who control vast sums of wealth. You may have heard the statistic that 2 percent of Americans control more than 60 percent of the country's entire net worth. On the other extreme, historically there is another percentage of Americans—about 2 percent—who live in abject poverty. Then there is the large middle class, so-called because these are the statistically "average" income earners. Another 10 or 15 percent fall right above or below "average," just as the bell curve predicts.

The reason I am going into such great detail here is that I believe the concept of the bell curve also has significant importance for you. The curve predicts that if you belong to a large company or work in a profession with a large number of others, there will be a percentage of very high achievers (typically, it will be roughly 2 percent of the group), with another 10 to 15 percent above average. But most people are indeed average producers.

In my all-day training programs, I always ask if there is anyone in the group who wants to be average with respect to income and productivity in their careers. No one ever raises their hand. If given a choice, I believe that nearly everyone would choose to be an "above average" performer: to make more money and live a better lifestyle. The fact of the matter is, you do have a choice. Most people tell me that they really don't aspire to be ultra-high achievers, but they certainly don't want to be average producers either. So let's look at the high achievers, at the upper third of the bell curve, and ask a very simple question. What are they doing that the average producers are not? Do they indeed share common characteristics, and can those characteristics be learned and duplicated?

If you interview virtually any high achiever in any profession, you are likely to find that they possess certain common characteristics. They are able to consistently produce high degrees of drive and determination because:

First, **they work very hard.** You simply do not bumble your way into high achievement. Top producers are often the first ones in the office in the morning and the last ones to go home at night. Top producers in sales don't have to be told to go pick up a telephone, because they are already making their calls.

Second, **they like what they are doing.** They have a personal commitment to their chosen profession. Different people like different things about their jobs. Some people like the income that their efforts produce. For others it is the intellectual challenge. But the bottom line is, it is difficult to stay driven if you really don't like your job.

Third, **they manage their time well.** They don't allow other people to waste their time. They recognize that time is their most precious commodity. And they organize their daily schedules effectively.

Fourth, *they are very creative in their approach to business and life.* These folks are always trying out new strategies, reading new books, taking classes, and learning new ways to improve themselves. They also tend to be very open-minded with respect to business. When presented with something new and different, they tend to readily accept it and try it out. Ultimately they may reject it as something that just doesn't work for them, but at least they try it with an open mind. This quality is extremely important in today's rapidly changing business climate.

Fifth, *they have a positive attitude.* Of course, a lot of people get this exactly backwards. They will say, "Of course they have a great attitude. I would have a great attitude too if I was making so much money." But when you talk to successful people, they tell you that the attitude came *before* the success.

Finally, *they regularly set goals and map out a strategy for achieving them.* They know where they are going and how they are going to get there. Ask these people where they see themselves five years down the road and they usually fire back a clear-cut, detailed answer. In fact, I believe the faster and more detailed the answer is, the more likely it is the person will actually reach their goals.

No doubt you've heard all this talk before about what makes someone successful. But there is another characteristic that most people never think about—and perhaps it is the most important one. A few years back, I used to ask successful people what they thought their "secret" to success was. I was surprised at how similar their answers were. In fact, many of their answers were identical. The secret they all had in common was best summarized by an advertising executive. He told me, "There is no secret to success. Anyone could be doing as well and making as much money as I am, if they really wanted to. The reason I do so well is I am willing to do what others won't do — and I do it every single day." It is really as simple as that. I've heard that statement from financially successful people dozens of times. Notice, they don't say, "I am doing what people *can't* do." They say they are doing the things that people *won't* do.

Successful people do what average producers won't do.

This point is so simple that people often miss it entirely. Let's say you are in sales. By far one of the simplest things you can learn to do to make your pathway to success easier is get in the habit of always asking for referrals. Yet the fact is that most people in sales ask for referrals only about half the time. This means that they are only generating roughly half the referrals of people who ask all of the time. The top achievers will tell you they have the same fears and anxieties and get the same knot in their stomach when it's time to ask the client for a recommendation — just like the average producers do. But somewhere along the line they have programmed themselves to always ask for referrals, and over time this results in a significant increase in their income. To understand this phenomenon statistically, let's refer back to the bell curve. About 2 percent of salespeople ask for referrals *all* of the time, while 68 percent ask *half* of the time, and one big reason that 2 percent of people in sales fail completely is that they *never* ask for referrals.

Put another way, if you are a salesperson who is currently asking for referrals roughly half the time, and if you could simply get yourself in the habit of asking *every single time,* how much additional income would you produce in the next year? This increase in income would be the direct result of your taking the time to program in that one simple behavior. Better still, how many tens of thousands in additional commission dollars would you generate in the next five years simply by going from a person who asks for referrals *some* of the time to someone who does it *100 percent* of the time?

This concept works well in every aspect of life. For example, top salespeople set appointments every day; average salespeople set appointments every other day; and people who fail in this business rarely, if ever, set appointments. Top salespeople have learned to ask for the sale at least five times, average salespeople ask once or twice, and many people fail as salespeople simply because they never learn how to ask for the sale. Many overweight people snack too frequently, people who are moderately overweight snack occasionally, and thin people listen to their bodies and rarely snack between meals.

What this all boils down to is the development of good business habits. It is the unconscious, habitual, rote behaviors you do every business day that are the single biggest determinants of where you will ultimately land in terms of income and productivity. With that in mind, let's discuss exactly how to internalize your daily goal.

5

Setting a Daily Goal

Earlier I asked you to write down one daily goal, one thing that you want to make sure gets done every day. The question is: Are you hitting that goal consistently? When I ask people in my audiences how often they actually achieve their daily goal, more often than not they say "about half the time." The main reason most people are mediocre performers is that they are hitting their daily goal only half the time, which places them squarely in the middle of the bell curve.

When I ask people why they fail to achieve their daily goal, they all have seemingly plausible excuses: their car broke down, their child was sick, they had a headache, they had a fight with their spouse, etc. In essence, these are all the same excuse. People who are not focused internally on the daily goal are easily distracted, and any out-of-the-ordinary event becomes a perfect excuse for them not to do what they need to do to achieve their goal.

Top achievers, however, also have cars that break down and kids that get sick. Yet they manage to reach their goal every single day. They often say that their business turned around the day they got it in their head that they were simply not going home until they reached the daily goal they set for themselves.

The daily goal acts as a benchmark for your success.

One top-producing executive told me his daily goal was the last thing he thought about before he went to sleep and the first thing he thought of when he woke in the morning. Sometimes his day would be a complete disaster, with all kinds of unexpected problems and interruptions. Yet he would still try to reach his daily goal. He said he knew that there would be good days and bad days in his business, but as long as he kept hitting his daily goal, he could predict with great accuracy where his business was likely to be three months, six months, and a year down the road.

People also report that setting and achieving a daily goal on a regular basis acts as a powerful stress reducer. By being able to predict numerically where your business is likely to be in the future, it takes away a lot of the everyday stress that comes with not knowing whether your next paycheck will pay the bills, and helps you to handle mundane everyday problems much better. This brings us to the question of exactly how to internalize these daily goals.

6

Kinesthetic Goal-Setting

Many people have told me that they truly desire to program in a daily goal, but simply don't know how. The good news here is that there really are quite a few methods of internalizing goals. As I stated earlier, I believe that if you recorded your goals on tape and listened to them every day for a month, you would internalize them auditorially. Also, if you learn to place yourself in a hypnotic state each day and visualize your goals, within 30 days you will have internalized these goals through the use of visual imagery. But there is another way that is often ignored: imbedding your goals kinesthetically by using things you already possess and use all of the time—your sensations and feelings.

The kinesthetic approach to goal-setting is predicated on three simple rules. The first rule is Pavlovian Theory: which is that any event followed by a pleasurable experience is likely to be repeated, while an event followed by a negative experience will tend to be avoided. This idea, also known as Classical Conditioning, or the Stimulus-Response Theory, is one of the bedrocks of modern psychological theory.

Rule number two is that it takes 21 to 30 days to create a new habit at the subconscious level. Of course, I did not invent this number. If you read *Think and Grow Rich* by Napoleon Hill, *The Power of Positive Thinking* by Norman Vincent Peale, *The Greatest Salesman in the World* by Og Mandino, or any other great motivational classics, you are likely to see this same concept discussed.

Please notice these books do not say it takes 21 years to get your head straight. It doesn't even take 21 weeks. Only 21 days—approximately one month! In other words, say your daily goal was to get yourself into the habit of scheduling three selling appointments per day, five days per week. And you made up your mind today that you were going to concentrate intently on this daily goal for the next 21 business days and not go home until you had scheduled those appointments. Well, by next month, if you stuck to your daily goal, you would find that this behavior came naturally. This is very good news.

What does this really mean? Let me give you a simple example. Let's say that, hypothetically, when you wake up tomorrow and got dressed, you decide to learn to tie your shoes in a different way. All of your life you've been tying your shoe using two loops, but now you decide you are going to learn to use only one loop. Try it and you will discover that, the first few times you do it, it feels awkward and uncomfortable. You have to look, think about it, force your hands to go in a way that they are not used to going. But, believe it or not, if you would do this every day for a month, within a month you wouldn't have to look anymore. The sheer act of repetition would drive the new information into your subconscious mind, and about one month later you would automatically and unconsciously tie your shoes in the new way. It would feel completely natural doing it like that, and then you would continue doing it like that until you reprogrammed yourself back to the old way.

In many respects, internalizing a daily goal is no different than learning to tie your shoes in a new way. Take a look at the daily goal you wrote down. Is it attainable? Could you achieve it every day for a month if you really wanted to? If you simply stay focused on your goal for one month, you can turn the behavior into a new unconscious habit. And, let's face it, one month is a relatively short period of time.

Most people say, "If that's all there is to it, why don't I go out and program myself to become the perfect businessperson?" Well, the reason most people don't succeed is rule number three: A bird in the hand is worth two in the bush. What I mean by that is for most people, motivation simply doesn't last for 21 days. If you remember, most people lose their motivation within 48 hours. And therein lies the dichotomy. It does not take long to produce a new unconscious habit—only about 21 days. Unfortunately, the drive, determination, and motivation that will get you there do not last nearly as long. So how can this problem be solved? One way is to attend a motivational seminar every 48 hours for the next month, which of course is not a very practical suggestion. Another way

> **If you simply stay focused on your goal for one month, you can turn the behavior into a new unconscious habit.**

would be to motivate yourself repeatedly over a 21-day period to keep your drive and motivation high enough to achieve the goal. So how could you remotivate yourself over and over within a 21-day period?

Here is what most people try to do: They set a goal and tell themselves that when the goal is achieved, they will earn a reward. But for most people, this simply does not work. Weight loss is an excellent example. An overweight person may set a goal of losing 50 pounds. When you ask them what the rewards of losing that weight will be, without hesitation they provide you with a long list. They explain how they will look better, feel better, wear clothes they haven't worn in years, and improve their health. The benefits are numerous and obvious. Yet you can go back two days later and you might find them eating a whole bag of potato chips. When you ask why they are not sticking to their diet, they often tell you what a tough day they were having or how nervous or bored they were. It turns out that the immediate gratification is often more powerful than the long-term rewards. This is true even though ultimately the long-term rewards far exceed the short-term gratification. In a nutshell, this is what I mean by "a bird in the hand is worth two in a bush."

Smoking behavior provides another vivid example of this concept. A smoker might wake up one morning with a hacking cough, throw the cigarettes down on the table, and say, "That's it! I quit!" Smokers often tell me that they don't even like smoking anymore. They will explain how it is a dirty, unhealthy, and expensive habit. Yet, when you run into them at the end of the day, they are contentedly puffing away. When you ask them what happened, they

> **If you don't see, feel, or touch the rewards for your efforts, within 48 hours you will probably lose most of your motivation toward achieving that goal.**

will tell you what a tough time they had, and how badly they needed a cigarette to get through the day.

I believe that setting goals in the business world is, in many respects, identical to setting personal weight-loss and smoking-cessation goals. The motivation is there at the beginning, but without a consistent set of rewards along the way the person can't make the behavior "stick." For example, companies often run sales contests where agents must produce all year in order to qualify. The actual prize isn't even awarded until six months later. That means the person needs to stay motivated for a full year in order to achieve the desired outcome and, for most people, that is simply unrealistic. Any psychologist is likely to tell you that what you can see, feel, and touch today is about 100 times more reinforcing than anything you have to wait for longer than 48 hours.

One final example. Let's say you give a command to your pet dog to sit, and the dog obediently responds. Most people would reward the animal either with a treat or a friendly pat on the head. The question is when you would reward the animal. Would you wait 30 seconds before giving the reward? Of course not. You would do it *immediately* because animals have very short attention spans. There is good news and bad news here. The good news is that our attention spans are somewhat longer than dogs'. The bad news is, not by a whole lot. If you cannot see, feel, or touch the rewards for your efforts, within 48 hours you will probably lose most of your motivation toward achieving that goal.

If this concept is still not very clear to you, think of the following. Let's say this book inspires you to go out and hit your daily goal this afternoon. If you do that, there will no doubt be long-term rewards for achieving that goal. But you may not see those rewards for weeks or even months. Your unconscious mind, however, needs to experience the rewards *as soon as possible* in order to stay motivated. What, then, could you reward yourself with on a daily basis? What could you give yourself, starting today, every day for the next month? How could you say to your unconscious mind, "This is what I've earned today, because I stayed focused on my goal"? Intellectually, you may know that by achieving your daily goal, six months or a year from now you could double or triple your income. But this is meaningless to your subconscious mind. It is best to think of your subconscious mind as an intelligent five-year-old: smart, but *very* impulsive. So what would you like as a daily reward? What would you be willing to work for today?

Here are some examples. A Realtor once told me, "I love music and I enjoy buying CD's, so whenever I am trying to develop a new habit, I put myself on a simple reward system. For a month, every day that I actually achieve my goal I stop at a music store on the way home

Most people have no accountability. There is nothing between them and the door.

from work and buy a new CD of my choice. It costs about $15 to purchase a new CD. Compared to the rewards of programming in the good habit, the good habit may be worth many times more than that CD. The subconscious mind can see and feel the CD *today,* and therefore it is a very effective motivator."

Perhaps there is something that you would really like to give yourself each day: a book, a magazine, a cassette? One woman told me that at the end of each day she would reward herself with one chocolate chip cookie. (Let me caution you, one chocolate chip cookie a day is a fine reward, but a box of chocolate chip cookies a day will cause a real problem!) One man told me that he really couldn't think of anything to give himself as a reward, but he worked in an office building where a florist was located. He decided that on each day where he reached his daily goal, he would buy one long-stemmed red rose for his wife. He reported to me that his wife really enjoyed getting the roses, and it became somewhat of a romantic ritual. Well, one day he failed to reach his goal so he went home without the rose. As he walked through the door, his wife noticed he was empty-handed. When he told her it was because he didn't reach his goal, she made him go back to the office and do it. Talk about reinforcement!

The point is, anything that will keep you focused on your goal long enough to turn it into a habit is beneficial. Right now, most people have absolutely no accountability. There is nothing between them and the door, so to speak. The end of the day comes, and they often realize that they have not done what they said they were going to do. And most people shrug their shoulders, chalk it up to a "bad day," and promise to try harder tomorrow. Of course, with no accountability, tomorrow's performance will be similar to today's and they never move beyond mediocre performance.

I propose that you put something between you and the door — a tangible reminder designed to refocus you on a daily basis and keep you motivated long enough to achieve your objective. So decide on a daily reward for yourself. It could be buying an inexpensive piece of hunting or fishing equipment or a new piece of clothing, giving yourself ten minutes of free time, taking a walk, receiving a massage, or perhaps getting your hair done or nails manicured.

Some people object that such rewards are too expensive. One woman told me that she enjoyed buying new clothes, but that a single blouse could easily cost $50. She said that if she spent $50 every day because she reached her goal, within a month she would be broke. So if your reward is really too expensive to give yourself on a daily basis, you may wish to utilize Plan B, which is called the "token system." Get a jar, dish, or glass, and earn tokens toward your reward. For example, each day you reach your goal, place a quarter in the jar and perhaps tell yourself when you have collected ten quarters you can go out and buy yourself a new shirt or blouse. Perhaps each quarter could represent $5; then three quarters could equal a new CD, or ten quarters a new golf club. Those of you who have children have probably already stumbled upon the token system. Often, my young son, Nicholas, will clean up his room if I promise to give him a gold star on the refrigerator. He enjoys earning those stars because they're tangible and immediate, and they don't cost me too much.

7

A "Punishing" Way to Achieve Your Goal

So far we have discussed how immediate rewards can help you stay focused long enough to reach your goals. It turns out that is only half of the equation. There are actually two parts to the formula for success. Any event followed by a pleasurable experience is likely to be repeated. But the flip side states that any event followed by a punishment will tend to be avoided. When was the last time you punished yourself? The last time you held yourself accountable for poor performance? Any parent soon learns that punishment is part of the process of being a responsible parent. If your child deliberately and willfully disobeys you, you would not ignore it. Yet when it comes to our business performance, we often do just that.

Here is what is meant by a punishment. Why not make a list of things you hate to do around the house? Things that would take 10 to 15 minutes to accomplish, but that really annoy you. And tell yourself that, starting today, every day you reach your goal you earn a reward, *and* every day you fail to reach your goal you make yourself do one of the "punishments" on that list. For example, the first day you fail to reach your goal, you have to wash

> **When was the last time you held yourself accountable for poor performance?**

the car before you eat dinner that night. Now washing the car may take you only 20 to 30 minutes and may not seem like a big deal. But if you are out there wet and hungry and it's 6:45 p.m., it might occur to you that it would have been easier to reach your goal at the office. One woman told me she hated organizing filing cabinets, so each day that she failed to reach her goal, she made herself take one drawer of the cabinet and organize it before she went home. She quickly learned to stay focused on her goal. Punishments might include washing the dishes by hand instead of putting them into the dishwasher. Another effective punishment might be to skip your favorite television program. It works for your children, so you might be surprised how well it works for you.

If you began to punish yourself for poor performance, you too would soon stay focused. A lot of people tell me they don't think this would work for them because they could never be conditioned by such a simple technique. But the fact of the matter is, we have already been conditioned hundreds of times before with precisely the same technique.

Wearing seatbelts is an excellent illustration. I used to despise wearing seatbelts. I felt that they were confining and uncomfortable. A few years back, the state I live in passed a law making it illegal not to wear your seatbelt. Yet I still drove without one quite often. At that time my eldest son, Michael, was nearly seven. Every time we would get in the car he would start saying, "Dad, you are not wearing your seatbelt." "Dad, you are breaking the law." "Dad, a police officer is going to stop you." Children sometimes have a great way of shaming you into doing the right thing! So each time I got in the car with him, I would make it a point to put my seatbelt on to set a good example. How many days do you think it took before I got in the habit of wearing a seatbelt? It took less than a month. It just doesn't feel right anymore to be driving in a car without wearing my seatbelt. I now feel uncomfortable without it. I have completely changed the way I view wearing a seatbelt. Chances are you may have had exactly the same experience. I learned to wear seatbelts from a basic reward-and-punishment system. Each time I refused to wear my seatbelt, my punishment was to hear my son go on and on about it. But when I put the seatbelt on there was an immediate reward — namely, he remained silent! It was real and tangible, it felt good, and it registered subconsciously.

Learning to drink diet soda is another illustration of how reward and punishment works. The first time many people tasted a diet drink, they didn't like it. It was not what they were used to, but they forced themselves to drink it because of the reward of saving so many calories. And they punished themselves with guilt when they drank the sugared version of the drink. Within 21 days of forcing themselves to drink the diet drink, most people learn to accept it, and many even learned to prefer its taste to the sugared drink. They will tell you the sugared drink tastes too sweet and syrupy.

Right now your daily goal may seem difficult and annoying. But if you simply stick with it, in a very short time your mind will learn to tune out any uncomfortable feelings and the daily goal will simply become part of your daily routine. It will become a good business habit, one that will contribute greatly to your ultimate long-term success.

8

Using Self-Hypnosis to Visualize Your Goals

The second pathway to the subconscious is the visualization technique. At this point I am going to begin using a term that is often misunderstood. That term is "trance." As I mentioned previously, a trance is actually a rather common state of mind. If you have ever driven past your exit on the freeway or become totally absorbed in a colorful daydream, you have experienced a trance. Have you ever called a member of your family for dinner and they were so absorbed on the computer that they didn't even hear you calling their name?

If you could follow someone for a full day and mea sure with a stopwatch how much time they spend conscious and in the here and now as opposed to a trance, you would rapidly see that most people spend far more time in a trance than out of one. For example, take a moment and see how much you can remember from your last drive into work. It may have been a thirty-minute drive or longer, but most people would be lucky if they could recall any more than four or five minutes of the total drive. That happens because most of the time that you are driving you are in a trancelike state.

The next obvious question is, "So what?" A man who heard me speak at a conference once said, "I never noticed it before, but I guess you are right. Your presentation made me realize how much of a given day I spend drifting in and out of reverie. But who cares? I seem to be doing all right." Well, here are two reasons you should care about whether or not you are in a trance.

First, it turns out that when you experience a trance, you tend to become much more malleable and open to suggestions. Have you ever seen what happens when a number of people are tranced out in front of a good TV program and one person in the room yawns? What happens is that everyone in the room begins to yawn. The suggestion to yawn goes straight into the subconscious, and each person responds before they have analyzed or criticized the thought. Advertisers spend billions of dollars looking for ways to deliberately put you into a trancelike state — captivating, colorful pictures, catchy tunes, sexy women, or handsome guys. Anything that captures your attention increases the impact of a commercial message.

The second reason you should be aware of how much time you spend in a trance is that while you are in a trance, you tend to be much more automatic and robot-like in your behaviors. Highway hypnosis is an excellent example of this phenomenon. Sometimes at the end of a business day, you get behind the wheel of your car, start the ignition, and simply tell your mind, "drive." Within a few moments one part of you is driving the car, but the other part is, as the saying goes, "a million miles away." Your subconscious mind is driving the car while you are consciously thinking of something else. Your subconscious is very programmable and will continue doing exactly what it is told to do until you tell it to stop. That is why it is so easy to drive past your exit on the freeway. You are so absorbed in your daydream that you don't even see the sign.

A young man once told me he was so absorbed in working on a business problem that he drove more than 100 miles out of his way. He got in the car in New York and only snapped out of it in Connecticut! He said what was so startling about the experience was that he had driven right up the New York Turnpike and had to have been paying tolls the entire way.

As you may have surmised, trancing on the highway is something you should *never* do. A Florida state trooper said he was always able to tell which accidents were the "highway hypnosis" cases because there were no skid marks on the road. People drove right off the road while in a trance. Do *not* practice self-hypnosis when you drive!

While you are in a trance, your unconscious mind will do exactly what you tell it to do until you snap out of your trance. This is true even if it is a self-destructive behavior. Chain-smoking is an excellent example of this. A smoker might enter a bar or a night club and purchase a pack of cigarettes. They have placed themselves in a dimly lit atmosphere, dulled their senses with some alcohol, and begun

> **Your subconscious will continue doing exactly what it is told to do until you tell it to stop.**

chain smoking as they became more and more absorbed in conversation. Two hours later, they reach down and notice the pack is empty, and that observation is what brings them out of their trance. Then comes the moment of realization. Could they really have smoked all of those cigarettes in just two hours? What is fascinating is that the smoker never would have done that if they were in a fully "conscious" state. If you had handed the cigarettes to that person and invited them to *try* to smoke them all within two hours, no doubt they would become sick halfway through the pack. But again, you will do whatever your unconscious mind tells you to do while you are in a trance.

Most people tell me they think they could never be hypnotized. In fact, statistically speaking, the opposite is true. It should be no surprise that, once again, hypnotic suggestibility is explained by the bell curve. Approximately 68 percent of a random group will be "average" hypnotic subjects. And all you need to internalize your goals, and successfully use this technique for self-improvement, is to be at least an average hypnotic subject. (Another 10 to 15 percent of a random group will be "very good" hypnotic subjects, with 2 percent being "excellent" subjects. This leaves only 10 to 15 percent of the group who are "poor" and 2 percent who are "very poor" subjects.)

You may have heard of people who go to a hypnotist in order to stop smoking. Some of them go once and then never touch a cigarette again. That actually does occur. Unfortunately, it happens only about 2 percent of the time. Most people could learn to change their habits and internalize their goals if they would simply practice one of the techniques in this book every day for at least 21 days. But expecting instantaneous results with these techniques is unrealistic. I have on occasion received phone calls from people who purchased my tapes or read an article that I had written, then practiced the technique and saw immediate results. However, such quick results are the exception rather than the rule. If you apply the techniques that were outlined in the previous chapters, you will see positive results over a reasonable period of time.

Another common misconception about being hypnotized is that you do not hear anything or that you are unconscious. In fact, you will always be aware of what is happening to you and will always hear what is going on. Self-hypnosis revolves around visualization and how to alter, in a positive way, what is known as your "subconscious self-image."

Many people talk about self-image, but few have given it any serious thought. Sometimes you may hear people say that they always do very well because they have such a positive self-image. Others are always getting themselves in trouble because they have such a poor self-image.

Our self-image has a powerful influence upon our beliefs and behavior. Most people earn exactly what their self-image tells them they deserve to earn, and end up exactly where their self-image tells them they deserve to be. So it stands to reason that, since your subconscious self-image is controlling your motivation, if you can change this picture you can also change the way you behave. In fact, a case could be made that, in order to permanently change behavior, you *must* change the picture. That is where self-hypnosis comes in.

Time and again, high achievers talk about their dream or their vision of success. Somewhere along the line they have taught themselves how to deliberately enter a state of focused awareness, and clearly and vividly visualize the goal they are trying to achieve. They do this repeatedly. Often you will hear them say that they go to bed every night and dream about becoming successful.

I believe that image is a very powerful thing and that it is affecting your behavior at a subconscious level in many different areas. First, let's find out what your self-image is. Take a moment, close your eyes and try to remember taking a bath or a shower. Admittedly this is a strange thing to do, but bear with me. Take a moment and remember.

When you recalled the image of taking a shower, didn't it include a picture of yourself in it? Wasn't it as if you had mentally removed yourself from your conscious mind, and you were looking at yourself standing in the shower or sitting in the bathtub? This, of course, is not the way it actually happened. If you were remembering it accurately, the way it really happened, all you would see in your mind's eye would be tiles on the wall, fixtures in the bathtub, and a shower curtain. That's the way it *actually* happened. But that was not the way you remembered it. That picture of yourself just came out of your subconscious mind.

Take a good look at that picture, because that is your self-image. That is what your subconscious mind thinks you look like in relation to the rest of the world around you. And that picture has some very powerful implications. For example, someone who pictures himself as an overweight person will most likely have a weight problem until he changes that picture, regardless of what diet he

> **Top producers can "see" themselves making a lot of money, and so time and again they do.**

tries. He can get on the world's greatest diet and drop 100 pounds. But if his subconscious mind still "sees" himself as overweight, he will probably gain the weight right back. Time and again, people with image problems experience the yo-yo effect of dieting. They lose the weight, gain it back, lose it again, and gain it back again.

Most people who lose weight and keep it off will tell you that part of the process was to change their inner picture of themselves. One client of mine reported that she once watched people going up to a buffet table. And she noticed that thin people saw food differently than she did. A thin person could walk up to a buffet table that had 30 different items, but they would focus on the salads, vegetables, and low-calorie, healthful foods. However, the overweight people walked up to the same table and often commented on the macaroni and cheese and chocolate cake. She said she was finally able to lose the weight and keep it off when she learned to look at food the way thin people did.

The same principles hold true in becoming more successful in your business. A lot of people say they want to make a lot of money and be high achievers, but they can't *see* themselves doing it. They are unconsciously focused on a mediocre goal; consequently, they rarely achieve anything exceptional. Recently, while giving a presentation, a sales manager pointed to a young salesperson in the audience and said that she was one of the most "natural" salespeople he had ever encountered. He described her as someone who had the gift of gab, a great personal presence, and good product knowledge. Later he told me that the woman had earned only $40,000 the previous year. When I asked why, he said it was because of the way she thought about herself. He pointed out that on a number of occasions he had talked with the young woman and urged her to set her sights higher, because she could easily have made double the income if she was more motivated. But the salesperson confessed she didn't think she was worthy of making more money.

So what happens to salespeople who focus on making $40,000 a year? Let's say in the first quarter of the year they do very well and earn $20,000. What do they do for the next three quarters? They pull back, goof off, and at the end of year they have made $40,000. Of course, the reverse is also true. If they have a terrible three quarters and only make $20,000 after those three quarters, then in the final quarter they will work overtime, increase their activity dramatically, and still wind up at the end of the year with $40,000. If you see yourself as a $40,000 producer, chances are you will make that kind of income. Top producers can "see" themselves making a lot of money, and so time and again they do. Their internal self-image is what drives them. And external factors—such as interest rates and the stock market—almost never affect them.

Speaking of income, there is a big difference between being "poor" and being "broke." Being broke is a temporary condition. Most of us at one time or another have been broke, but we always tend to bounce back to the economic level where we think we belong. Being poor, on the other hand, can be the result of a subconscious self-image. You could give a poor person $100,000 in cash, then come back a year later, and that person might still be poor. They might have a new car in the driveway or some fancy new clothes. But chances are they would be living in the same neighborhood, spending time with the same people, eating in the same restaurants, and doing the same things for leisure and recreation. The government is unlikely to ever truly eliminate poverty in this country until the effects of self-image are taken into account.

What would happen if you had all of your money and possessions taken away from you? Imagine that as of today, all you had were the clothes on your back and the knowledge inside your head. Chances are, within a year—two years at the most—you would be right back to living in the kind of neighborhood you are used to living in, buying your clothes in the same stores, and doing the same things for leisure and recreation. The economy does not control that; your clients do not control that. This is an example of the control of your subconscious self-image.

Examples of Visualization

Former National Football League star Brian Holloway is a friend of mine. After playing at Stanford University, he was All-Pro five years in a row for the New England Patriots. He described a technique he learned at Stanford from one of his defensive coaches. Every Monday the team would have to learn new defensive plays for the upcoming game Saturday afternoon. They would spend all afternoon on the practice field, and then the coaches would take them back to the gym and have them lie on mats on the gym floor. The coach said, "You just spent all day running the plays out on the field. Now I want you to run them in your mind." Every day they would run the plays 25 times in their minds. Brian said that he really enjoyed this time. He would get very relaxed and actually see himself making the tackles. The net result was that by the day of the big game, he had already run the plays 125 times in his head. Going out and actually doing it on Saturday afternoon was simply the 126th time.

Not long ago, I was talking to a manager of a mid-sized insurance agency in Long Island, New York. This man had just taken over the agency and was discussing ways to build its sales. He told me that his group did about $1 million a year in premium sales, but they were surrounded by agencies that did many times that. There was an agency in New York City, for example, that did $12 million. He told me that when he decided to take over his agency, he began visualizing himself managing a $5-million-dollar-a-year agency within three years. Each night before he would drift off to sleep, he would try to see himself hiring good, productive agents and managing them into successful careers. In his mind he would go over how he was going to write the newspaper ads to recruit these people. He would see himself at job fairs attracting the best and the brightest. In fact, he told me that in his head he already had the $5-million-dollar agency built. Going out and actually putting the pieces together was almost like a mere formality.

Recently I was the keynote speaker for the annual awards banquet of a large sales organization. The big award of the night was the "Agent of the Year." When it was announced, the winner walked up to the podium. He paused for a moment, and then turned to the previous year's winner and said, "Last year when you won the award, I was sitting in the audience. I made up my mind at that moment that I was going to be the winner this year. Every night before I went to bed, I would close my eyes and try to imagine what it was going to feel like standing up here at the podium giving my acceptance speech, and here I am at last!"

The previous descriptions of visualization are excellent examples of self-hypnosis. Most people think that when you are in trance you are unconscious and unaware of what is going on around you. In fact, all of those little daydreams and all of that mental drifting are trancelike states. Let's now discover how to put them to good use.

There is an art and a technique to visualization that can be easily learned with just a little bit of practice. The first part of any visualization process is to learn how to give your subconscious mind visual suggestions. When deciding what to focus on with self-hypnosis, it is important **The subconscious is extremely literal in its interpretation.** that you be as specific as possible. To say that you want to be more successful or make a lot of money is simply too vague. But to say "Within three years, I will be making an income of $250,000 and be an executive vice president in my company" is clear and specific. The subconscious is extremely literal in its interpretation.

Take a moment right now and raise your right hand. Most people who do this raise their right arm and their right hand. However, if you suggest the same thing to a hypnotized person, they will raise only the hand. The subconscious mind does exactly what you ask it to. If you repeatedly suggest to yourself that you will make more money next year than this year, you may end up with $5 more, but that is probably not what you intended.

It is also important that your suggestions be as vivid as possible. There is a formula in self-hypnosis that you should be aware of: $I \times V = R$, where I is the image, V is the vividness, and R is the amount of response.

For example, if you were to close your eyes and form a picture of a slice of lemon, the picture itself would probably produce little or no physical response. However, if you closed your eyes and imagined yourself taking a bite out of a tart, bitter, juicy slice of lemon, and you could taste the lemon juice squirting into the back of your mouth, at that moment you would probably be experiencing an increase in your salivary response.

When visualizing your goals, you want to make them as bright, clear, and vivid as possible, and this may take some practice. It is not uncommon for people to report that they needed repeated sessions before they felt they could visualize their goals clearly. The more you practice this the better you will get, so do not be discouraged.

It may be helpful to take a few minutes at this point and investigate just how you visualize. The human brain has an almost astounding capacity to form, hold, and process visual imagery. Some people compare the brain to a computer, but it is infinitely more complex than any computer in existence. Close your eyes for a moment and form a picture of your vehicle. You will probably find that you have absolutely no problem doing this instantly. Of all of the billions of memories and images in your mind, you can instantly access virtually any one of them with no effort whatsoever. We refer to these as mental pictures, yet they are much more similar to holograms.

For example, close your eyes and bring back that picture of the vehicle you drive. If you imagine that your mind is like a camera with a zoom lens, and simply will the picture to get larger and larger, that is exactly what happens. Next, imagine that you are backing away from the picture. Tell it to get smaller and smaller until it almost disappears. Then imagine yourself looking at the vehicle from different angles. See yourself standing in front of the vehicle looking at the windshield and hood. Next, imagine yourself standing behind it looking at the rear window and trunk. Pretend you are floating above it, looking down on the roof, and then imagine that you are lying on the ground, looking up at it. Next, bring it back to its original angle and begin changing its color. In your mind paint it green, then paint it red, then paint it purple, then paint it yellow. Now put blue polka-a-dots all over it.

This simple experiment should illustrate how wonderfully rich and complex the process of visual imagery is. As you repeatedly visualize your goals, you will find that they become both more clear and more vivid to you. And the more vivid they are, the more likely you are to get the desired response.

In the following paragraphs you are going to learn an excellent technique for inducing a trancelike state. Before you practice the self-hypnosis, you want to decide which goal you are going to visualize. Pick one clear-cut, specific goal at a time. It is possible to change a variety of behaviors with visualization, but you do not want to try to change them all simultaneously. A client once came into my office with a shopping list. He wanted to stop smoking, lose weight, control his back pain, *and* double his income! If he prioritized his goals and spent at least 30 days focusing on each of them, one at a time, it is entirely conceivable that he would see positive results in all of the desired areas. But by trying to accomplish them all simultaneously, he would likely see diminished effects.

What you are trying to do here essentially is focus your unconscious mind. After you have chosen a specific goal and are in the trance state, you want to use your imagination and visualize the desired goal as if it has already occurred. You want to see yourself looking and feeling the way you want to be once the goal has been attained. You want to visually suggest to your unconscious mind exactly the way you want to look and precisely the way you want to feel. Hold that image for as long as you can (which initially may be only a few seconds). If your mind wanders, keep bringing it back to the goal. Over time the wandering will stop, you will be able to clearly visualize the goal continuously, and at that point you will be truly experiencing the hypnotic state.

As your body becomes more relaxed and you begin to enter the trance state, at least initially you are probably going to want to test to see if you are in a trance state. Sometimes the physical sensations associated with trancing —such as a drifting, floating, or sinking feeling—are so obvious you will know that a change is taking place. More often than not, however, there is little or no physical sensation associated with the trance. So the only way you will know if it is happening is to give yourself a suggestion and measure the results. Before we get to that, it's time to learn how to mentally and physically relax.

9

A Relaxing Way to Succeed

We live in a high-paced world where people tend to be active from the minute they wake up to the minute they go to sleep. If you are truly serious about learning self-hypnosis, the first recommended step is that you devote five uninterrupted minutes each day for the next 21 days, just learning how to relax completely.

In the early 1920s a researcher named Hans Seyle conducted a series of ground-breaking experiments studying the effects of stress. In one of these experiments, he was looking at the effects of *physical* stress on an organism. In order to create physical stress he raised a series of lab rats in cages that had electrified grids on the floor. Periodically and without warning, he sent an electrical current through the shock grid. As you might imagine, these unexpected shocks on the animals' naked feet were very stressful to them. After the animals matured, they were sacrificed and autopsies were performed on them. Seyle then listed a whole series of findings as to the effects of that physical stress on the body. He found hardening of the arteries, enlargement of the heart, elevated levels of a number of hormones and brain chemicals, increased acid levels in the stomach, and a number of changes to other organs in the body.

His next series of experiments were designed to look at the effects of *psychological* stress on the body. In order to do this he raised a series of laboratory rats in cages placed directly next to cats in cages. This, of course, was extremely stressful psychologically to the rats. When the animals matured, they were sacrificed, autopsied, and compared to a control group. Much to Seyle's surprise, the results were nearly identical to the physically stressed rats. The psychologically stressed group showed the same hardening of the arteries, enlarged heart, elevated hormone levels, etc. These findings and others led Seyle to conclude that psychological stress can be every bit as destructive to the body as physical stress under certain circumstances. These circumstances, however, appear to vary from individual to individual.

In the 1970s the Federal Aviation Administration conducted a study of air traffic controllers. The purpose of the study was to try and find out why some air traffic controllers were experiencing stress-related problems such as high blood pressure, insomnia, and migraine headaches, while others did not. Up until that point there were no satisfactory explanations for this discrepancy. In fact, based on the hiring practices for air traffic controllers, it was predicted that there would be no variations with respect to how they handled job stress. This was because before air traffic controllers are hired, they are extensively screened for psychological and physical suitability. There is a very narrow range of acceptance for such an important job and certain clearly defined criteria have to be met.

On paper these individuals appeared to be very similar in terms of psychological makeup and physical condition. Yet, as soon as three years later, some of them were suffering from extensive physical problems associated with stress whereas others were completely unaffected.

The FAA study took four years, cost millions of dollars, and ultimately concluded the following: The single biggest determinant as to whether an air traffic controller was going to experience physical stress-related problems on the job was the way they *perceived* what they were doing. When asked how they viewed their jobs, some of the controllers emphasized the level of responsibility they were given, how they had to make life-and-death decisions on a regular basis, and how aware they were that if they made a mistake, it could cost hundreds of people their lives. Other controllers, when asked the same question, reported that they learned to look at the blips on the radar screen like a big game. One controller went so far as to claim that he thought of his job like a big "Pac-man" game — to make sure the plane didn't get gobbled up.

There was a direct correlation between the number of stress-related problems in the group that saw themselves in a stressful, high-risk, and potentially deadly situation as opposed to the group that was able to mentally detach themselves from that aspect of their job. Clearly, the way we perceive a situation has a lot to do with whether we will experience stress from it or not.

Psychological stress can be as every bit as destructive to the body as physical stress.

When an organism is placed under stress, the body is goes on alert. The heart rate increases, the muscles tense, blood pressure goes up, and adrenaline begins to flow at a rapid rate. This is a natural defense mechanism and is completely adaptive. A problem occurs if the person is under stress for too long. These defensive mechanisms begin to tire and break down. If a person is under stress for too long, they actually become susceptible to certain diseases. They may experience stress-related medical problems such as tension headaches, nervous stomachs, fatigue, and even some forms of asthma. The body, however, has tremendous recuperative powers. If given the opportunity, it will rejuvenate itself very effectively.

Periodic breaks in the stress level are needed for the body to be able to reconstruct itself. In the high-paced world in which we live today, many people rarely relax. From the moment we get up until the moment we fall asleep, there are demands placed on our time. We awaken to the sound of an alarm clock or buzzer and are

> **Periodic breaks in the stress level are needed for the body to be able to reconstruct itself.**

immediately following a tight schedule. Many people start their day by ingesting caffeine or nicotine and then getting behind a wheel of a car. We don't think of it that much, but driving an automobile requires on the average four life-or-death decisions per minute. When you arrive at the office, more often than not you are confronted with a series of stressful problems lasting throughout the day. Then the person drives home again, ingests a meal laced with chemicals and preservatives, and proceeds to sit in front of a television set and watch programs filled with sex and violence. Often the person does this day in and day out without ever allowing their body to relax and regenerate. It's no wonder heart attacks are the number one killer in this country.

But it does not take long for the body to recover from this stress. The studies are quite clear that virtually any kind of organized stress-reduction activity will go far to ameliorate most of the negative aspects of this stress. The key is that the stress reduction must be done on a regular basis and you have to learn to *really* relax when you do it. Some people go on a vacation with their cell phone, laptop computer, and office work—never truly leaving the stress behind.

How to Hypnotize Yourself

Without a doubt, practicing self-hypnosis is one of the best stress reduction activities you can learn. It is quite simple, can be done almost anywhere, and within three weeks you will see positive results. After having trained literally thousands of people in this technique, I can state without hesitation that if you follow this exercise, within 30 days you will notice the following effects: an increased ability to concentrate, more energy, and a more relaxed feeling during the day. Chances are that you will also sleep better during the night after using this technique. The technique is as follows.

Pick a place where you are not likely to be disturbed. Lock the door, take the phone off the hook, send the kids out to play. Get into a comfortable position, either lying or sitting down. Make sure that your feet and your legs are uncrossed. Close your eyes and begin breathing slowly and deeply. As you inhale, slowly count from one to five. Then hold your breath and slowly count again from one to five. As you exhale, slowly count from one to ten. If you do this three times, by the end of the third breath your body will be well on its way to relaxing completely.

It also helps tremendously if you imagine in your mind that you are breathing through the bottoms of your feet. When you are inhaling, imagine that you are breathing through the soles of your feet, and when you are exhaling, imagine that you are letting go of the tension.

Next, mentally go through each part of your body, starting with your feet, and allow that part to become thoroughly and completely relaxed. Use your imagination and visualize the muscles becoming limp and loose and totally unwound. As you do this, you may begin to notice a tingly or numb sensation. This is completely natural. Tell yourself that is the tension draining from your body.

Invite the relaxation to continue spreading up through your legs. When every muscle from your waist down is totally relaxed, pause for a moment and enjoy the sensation. Then invite the muscles in your stomach, back, shoulders, and chest to become completely relaxed. Feel the relaxation spreading down through your arms and hands and into your fingers until your entire body from your neck down is totally and completely relaxed. At this point many people report feeling a drifting, floating, or even sinking sensation. You may begin to feel as if you are falling asleep. All of this is perfectly natural. Finally, invite the muscles in your face, jaws, forehead, temples, head, and scalp to totally relax.

At this point, once again, you want to use your imagination. Imagine you are standing at the top of a staircase which is five steps high. At the bottom of the staircase, in your mind's eye you can see a large white bed with a soft white pillow. In your mind begin slowly counting backwards from five down to one. And imagine that with each number, you are traveling one step down the staircase, getting one step closer to that bed. By the time you reach the number one, you are lying in that soft white bed with your head on that soft white pillow in a very deep, sound, and peaceful relaxation. Your subconscious should now be ready to receive positive suggestions from your conscious mind.

Testing Your Trance

As mentioned earlier, you may not feel as if you are hypnotized, so you may wish to give yourself a test to tell you whether your subconscious mind is responding. There are many such tests, but the following two are the easiest to learn and most effective.

Eye Closure: By far the most commonly used test of hypnosis is eye-closure. Once you have allowed yourself to become completely relaxed mentally and physically, imagine that you can feel your eyelids growing heavier and heavier. You may wish to imagine that they are filling with lead or stuck tightly together with glue. Within a moment or two, you should actually feel them getting heavier. Allow this sensation to develop for approximately

30 seconds. Then mentally tell yourself that as you count back from three to one, with each number your eyelids will grow heavier still, and by the time you reach the number one your eyelids will feel so relaxed and heavy it will be impossible to open them. As you slowly count backwards in your mind, really try to feel the heaviness. As you reach the number one, go ahead and try to open your eyes. If the suggestion has reached your subconscious mind, you will discover that they simply will not open no matter how hard you try.

If they easily pop open with no resistance at all, do not despair. It sometimes takes five or six sessions before a person begins to enter the trance state. And if you keep practicing, at some point you will discover that your eyelids really are locked tightly together. Not being able to open your eyelids is a signal from your subconscious mind that the suggestions you are giving it are being received. At that point, you would begin to give yourself whatever suggestions for self-improvement you wish.

Arm Levitation: Another test for hypnosis is known as arm levitation. Once you have become deeply relaxed, focus on one of your arms. Use your imagination and see a string tied around your wrist. The string is tied to a giant balloon filled with helium gas. See the balloon clearly and vividly in your mind, and begin to tell yourself that you can feel your arm and hand getting lighter and lighter.

After approximately 60 seconds of visualizing this, you will begin to notice your arm and your hand first feeling tingly and numb, and then getting lighter and lighter. If the suggestions are reaching your subconscious mind, your arm will soon feel so light it will actually begin to lift and float right up into the air. If your arm feels light, but not light enough to actually float, you may wish to imagine that you are tying more and more balloons to your arm. When the arm floats, it should be effortless. In other words, you are not physically lifting it; it feels as if it is rising all by itself.

When you can get your arm to float autonomously, you can rest assured that your subconscious mind is receiving your suggestions and you are ready to give yourself positive, productive suggestions for self-improvement.

How to Give Yourself Suggestions

Now that you're in a peaceful, relaxed, trancelike state, your subconscious mind is more receptive to suggestions. You will also find that your imagination tends to be much more clear and vivid. Take a moment and imagine that you are being transported forward to a time after you have already accomplished your goal. Form a bright, clear picture of yourself looking exactly how you want to look and feeling exactly how you want to feel. As you see this picture, tell yourself this is how you want to look and feel.

Do your best to focus on that picture for at least two uninterrupted minutes. And then tell yourself, as you slowly count forward from one to five, that by the time you reach the number five your eyelids will be wide open and you will be wide awake, feeling refreshed, relaxed, and in complete and total control. If you practice this technique at night before you go to bed, you may wish to simply continue relaxing until you fall into a deep and peaceful sleep.

Essentially, that is the complete technique of self-hypnosis. Try devoting five minutes each day to relaxing and visualizing your goals. Don't be surprised if your mind tends to wander during the first few sessions. Many people report that it was not until the fifth or sixth session that they felt their mind calm down and they were able to continually focus for more than 15 to 20 seconds at a time.

If possible, it's best to practice this technique at the same time each day. In other words, if you are going to visualize first thing in the morning, do it every day first thing in the morning. If you choose to practice before you fall asleep, then do it every night before you fall asleep. This sets up a regular pattern which your unconscious mind will quickly pick up on.

Scripts for Use During Visualization

The following is a series of scripts which you may want to repeat to yourself while practicing your visualization technique. Repeating these scripts to yourself during self-hypnosis will deepen the trance and speed up the results. Feel free to expand on or modify these statements to meet your specific needs.

Stress Reduction

1. I am relaxed and in complete control at all times.

2. I sleep peacefully at night and awaken relaxed and refreshed.

3. Each day it becomes easier and easier for me to enjoy the benefits of being completely relaxed.

4. Relaxation is a natural state of my body.

5. My body and mind are working together to remain focused and relaxed.

Motivation

1. I am highly motivated at all times.

2. Each day I am becoming more and more energetic and focused on my goals.

3. I enjoy setting goals and accomplishing them.

4. As I get closer and closer to my goals, I feel better and better.

5. Setting goals is fun and I do set goals.

6. I enjoy spending time with highly motivated individuals.

7. Each day I am becoming more and more motivated.

Attitude

1. I have a positive and prosperous mental attitude.

2. I look for the good in situations and I always find it.

3. My life is interesting and I am prosperous.

4. I make a conscious effort to surround myself with other positive individuals.

5. My mind is filled with positive, productive thoughts.

Overcoming Procrastination

1. I have a "do it now" attitude

2. I get the job done on time or before.

3. The sooner I get the job done, the sooner I reap the rewards.

4. As I get closer and closer to completing the task, I feel better and better.

5. I start my work without hesitation and with complete confidence.

Successful Selling

1. I enjoy connecting with my prospects.

2. My product has value and I am helping my clients by selling it to them.

3. The more I sell, the more successful I am becoming in my business.

4. I sell with complete confidence and enthusiasm.

5. Selling something I believe in is easy to do.

10

The Auditory Technique

The third internalization technique is the auditory approach to goal-setting: namely, getting your goals on tape. How many hours a week do you spend driving around in your car? These days most automobiles come equipped with a tape player built into the dashboard. If you would simply take some time to write down your goals, turn them into a series of affirmations, and then verbally record them onto a cassette tape, you would have another extremely powerful approach to goal-setting.

If you played your goal tape once a day every day for 21 days, the act of repetition would drive the information on the tape deep into your subconscious mind. One thing is certain: you would know your goals inside and out.

This process is similar to the way in which television and radio commercials become ingrained in your mind. The average American can spit back hundreds of commercial jingles with little or no conscious thought. You can say to someone "Please don't squeeze..." and they'll automatically respond with "...the Charmin." Have you ever wondered why advertisers spend billions of dollars doing that to you? Advertising obviously has an effect on behavior. And one of the most profound effects is a subtle yet very powerful change in your perception.

You were just reminded of the Charmin commercial. Whether you like it or not, since I focused you on it, you are still subconsciously thinking about it and will continue to think about it for at least the next 48 hours. Which means if you find yourself in a supermarket within the next couple of days and push your cart down the aisle with the bathroom tissue, even though there may be 20 different brands of tissue, all with brightly colored packaging and all competing for your attention, which one will you notice first? Chances are, because you are subconsciously focused on the Charmin commercial, you will tend to see that brand first. And when you do, you are likely to have what is called an "impulse response." You may catch yourself mumbling, "Please don't squeeze it," or "It's squeezably soft," or see the picture of the Mr. Whipple character in your mind. Advertisers know that if they can do that to you—have you consciously looking at a product while you are subconsciously thinking about buying it—the likelihood of you acting on that thought goes up dramatically.

Once you focus on something, the way you see and perceive things changes almost instantly. Have you ever purchased a new automobile, and all of the sudden it looks like the world is filled with exactly the same car you just bought? You buy a new car and it looks like everybody and their brother is driving around in the same vehicle. The model you just bought has been around for years, but you probably never paid much attention to it.

Once you focus on something, your perception changes almost instantly.

However, the day you buy one, you suddenly can't help but notice that you are seeing the same car everywhere. That's what happens when your mind gets focused. When my wife Cathy was pregnant with our first child, Nicholas, I couldn't go into a shopping mall without noticing dozens of pregnant women.

The same psychology influences whether or not you will achieve your goals this year. Once you take the time to internalize a goal, you will start to perceive situations differently. You will see people you meet in all kinds of encounters in a completely new way. Salespeople who get focused on appointments and referrals see the telephone in a totally different way. The more focused you are on asking for referrals, the more likely you will be to see the client as a source of good, quality leads. The more focused you are on reaching your goal, the more likely you will be to reach it.

Put simply, the more focused you are on appointment-setting, the more likely you will be to notice the telephone on your desk when you sit down. If you work from a desk, you can determine where your focus is by noticing where you have placed the telephone. People who are not focused on making phone calls will often place the telephone as far away from them as they can. And that is usually up and off in the corner away from their visual field. Right in the middle of their desk are the visual distractions such as an empty coffee cup, newspaper, or pamphlets to read.

Many "unfocused" producers notice the coffee cup first and immediately think "I'll go and get a cup of coffee before I start setting appointments." Then they notice the newspaper and read that for a few minutes, etc.

So, you see that the key to achieving your goals is to remain focused on them. This is something you already have the capacity to do. We know this is true because you already are programmed in countless ways that require no effort on your part. It will not take long for you to program yourself to have winning business habits that will help you achieve what you want to achieve.

Here is an excellent example of how putting goals on tape could change your behavior. Suppose every day on the way into work a salesperson takes a tape out of her glove compartment and pops it into the tape player. Soft music begins to play and every ten seconds or so she hears her own voice repeatedly saying, "I enjoy working on the telephone. The telephone is my vehicle to success. When I sit down at my desk I immediately reach out and pick up the telephone. I like working on the telephone." If that person listened to this tape every day for the next 21 days, when she sat down at her desk, would she be more likely to notice the empty coffee cup, the newspaper, or the telephone? And when she saw the telephone, what would she start thinking? At that point, it is much more likely that she will pick up the telephone and start making phone calls, as opposed to wasting time.

Another example of how useful this technique can be is learning to ask for referrals. Many people who should ask for referrals in business are not comfortable doing so.

So they simply wipe it out of their mind. Suppose every day for the next three weeks, while a salesperson drank his morning coffee and read his newspaper, he had a tape playing in the background with his own voice repeatedly saying, "I enjoy asking for referrals. Asking for referrals is the smart thing to do. Asking for referrals helps me improve my business. I always remember to ask for referrals." Twenty-one days later do you think that person will keep forgetting to ask for referrals?

Overeaters can create a tape that says, "I prefer foods that are good for me. I enjoy eating foods that are low in calories ..." etc.

The beauty of this technique is that it is custom-designed. Your goal tape can be exactly what you want to focus on, with your own goals and in your own voice. Now let's look at how to actually make these tapes.

The first step is to create a detailed goal script. You are going to want to refer back to the goals you wrote down earlier and decide which of these goals you want to use on your goal tape. Let's say you decide to make a tape that emphasizes your 30- to 90-day goal. Begin by breaking the goal down into its component parts. For example, if your goal is to make $25,000 in income in the next 90 days, you might deduce that in order to achieve that goal you need to:

- Pick up the phone at least 20 times every afternoon,

- Spend at least an hour and a half each morning doing paperwork,

- Go and see at least three people face-to-face every afternoon,

- Always ask your clients for at least three good referrals, and

- Send out at least 100 pieces of targeted mail each week.

This becomes the overall strategy that you must employ in order to actually achieve your goal. Now that you have a goal and a strategy to achieve that goal, you want to begin developing properly written affirmations.

Making Your Script

An affirmation is a direct statement to your unconscious mind. Properly written affirmations possess certain characteristics. Affirmations should always be written in the present tense. You don't want to tell your mind what you *will* do, *should have* done, or are *going to* do. The only thing your subconscious mind will respond to is what you *are* doing.

Typically, affirmations should emphasize the positive. You probably don't want to tell your unconscious mind that smoking is dirty or that it causes cancer. It is much more productive to emphasize the benefits of not smoking: that you will feel better, be healthier, and save a lot of money. Affirmations should also be emotional in nature. Emotion is one of the sensitizers of the human brain. If you saw a bad car accident, you would not have to try to remember the event. The emotion fixates your attention and sends the information straight to the subconscious mind. Anyone old enough to remember the Kennedy assassination remembers exactly where they were and what they were doing when they heard the news. You should frame your emotions in a positive way to sensitize your brain. For example, you might say, "I love reaching the goal. I get excited when I reach the goal..." etc.

Your affirmations should emphasize how you will feel having achieved your goal. Tell yourself that you can hear people complimenting you, that you can see yourself looking the way you want to look, etc. The following are some sample affirmations. You may wish to simply copy them down and fill in the appropriate blanks. G is the goal you are trying to achieve, D is the deadline which you intend to achieve it by, and A is the specific activity that will take you to your goal.

Sample Scripts

1. My daily goal is (G) _____.

2. My mid-range goal is (G) _____.

3. My long-term goals are (G) _____
    _____.

4. I am achieving my goal of (G) _____
    by (D) _____.

5. I see myself doing (A) _____ as my
    goal of (G) _____ is completed
    by (D) _____.

6. I feel great doing (A) _____
    because it helps me to accomplish my goal of
    (G) _____ by (D) _____.

7. The sweet smell of success is mine when I do
    (A) _____ as I get closer and closer to
    (G) _____ by (D) _____.

8. I enjoy listening to my goal tape every day because it
    ensures that I reach my goal of (G)_____
    by (D)_____.

9. When I do (A)_____, my goal of
    (G)_____ becomes more clear and
    vivid in my mind.

Once you have your script prepared, you will need a
tape player, a tape recorder, and a blank tape. On the tape
player, put some soft, pleasant, rhythmic music. Studies
have shown that soft music helps create a physical state
of relaxation and speeds up the learning process. Any
type of soft music will do, but it is generally agreed that
classical music containing a largo rhythm with 60 beats
per minute gives the best results. Examples of this type of
music would be Bach's *Brandenburg Concertos,* Pachelbel's
Canon in D, and Vivaldi's *Four Seasons.* The most important thing is that the music be pleasant and rhythmic in
nature.

Affirmations should emphasize the positive.

Start playing the music in the background at moderate volume. Then take your hand-held tape recorder and place a blank tape in it. Press the Record button so that the music coming out of the tape player is being picked up by the hand-held tape recorder. You should have your script in your hand and, while the music is playing, begin to read your affirmations into the tape recorder at roughly ten-second intervals in a clear and enthusiastic manner. Read the affirmations over and over until you have filled up at least 10 to 15 minutes of tape. At the end of this process, you will have your goals on tape in a very personalized way.

Now comes the easy part. One of the advantages of this process is that you don't even have to concentrate on the tape. You don't have to pull your car over to the side of the road and pay close attention to what is being said. You weren't concentrating on all of those radio and television commercials playing in the background, yet they are buried in your subconscious mind. The same is true here. If you simply have the tape playing in the background every day for the next 21 days, your subconscious mind will pick up the messages on the tape, passively, with little or no effort on your part.

If you do not like listening to tapes in your car or it doesn't have a tape player, you can have the tape playing in the background while you are doing paperwork in the office, working out, gardening, walking, or virtually any activity at all. As your subconscious repeatedly hears the affirmation, it will become more and more focused on the message and thus more likely to initiate the activity needed to get you there.

The Meaning of It All

At this point, it is important to step back and ask yourself, "Why exactly am I setting and trying to achieve these goals?" In the high-paced world in which we live, some people pursue an objective and really have no idea of the meaning behind the pursuit. A goal, after all, is just a frozen instant in time. If you wanted to make a lot of money, you might set as an objective the goal of making one million dollars. If you work very hard toward it, in all likelihood at some point you would indeed be worth one million dollars.

A goal is just a frozen instant in time.

There would come a moment when you would have achieved the goal. However, if the pursuit is just to make a lot of money, the next obvious goal would be to be worth two million dollars, then three, then four, etc. A pursuit without meaning is like running on a treadmill—a lot of activity, but very little forward motion.

Many people who exhibit Type A behavior suffer from this syndrome. There is no real purpose behind their pursuit of a goal, so they just keep going faster and faster, trying harder and harder, and never seem to be able to feel true satisfaction or contentment.

In fact, in our culture, this meaningless pursuit often follows a very definable three-phase process. First, we are conditioned to believe that having "more" will produce greater satisfaction. If only we had more money, more possessions, more thrills, or more love, that would make us feel happy and fulfilled. Yet, if you talk to very rich individuals or celebrities, expecting that they would have most of everything that life has to offer, they are often the first to tell you that more, in and of itself, does not provide true happiness or contentment. There are seemingly endless stories of famous, rich people who have died of a drug overdose or gone through multiple divorces.

Many people never get out of the first phase. They endlessly pursue "more" and generally die completely unfulfilled, wondering why life seemed so meaningless and empty to them. However, if they do get out of the "more" phase, the next thing they tend to do is reason, "Well, if 'more' didn't make me happy, 'better' certainly will." They pursue the best of everything: to eat in the best restaurants, have the best car, spend time with the best people, and have their children attend the best schools. In order to discover how futile this pursuit is, simply ask someone who has the best of everything—a Kennedy or a Rockefeller, for example—if the best of everything in and of itself makes them feel any happier or more fulfilled. They are likely to tell you that it is certainly nice to have the best, but having the best does not make you sleep better at night, improve your relationship with your loved ones, or make you feel like more of a person.

Once again, some people never get out of their meaningless pursuit of "better." But if they do, they are likely to enter the next and most dangerous phase. They begin to deduce, "If 'more' didn't make me happy, and 'better' didn't make me feel any better about myself, perhaps, 'different' is the answer." They enter what is commonly referred to as a mid-life crisis. "Maybe if I had a different job I would be happier. Perhaps a different spouse would give me more satisfaction. What if I lived in a different place?" At this point, some people get very strange. And of course, the problem with different is that, in this culture, you are not permitted to get very different before people begin suggesting medication or even locking you up.

A friend of mine once pointed out that in our society you could walk into a hotel lobby, sit down, and cry all day long, and no one would be likely to bother or harass you. Yet, if you walked into the same lobby and began laughing hysterically, within an hour they would probably lock you up. There are certain behaviors in this culture that are not tolerated. Many people who go through a mid-life crisis start behaving in very strange ways: they quit their jobs, change their appearance, disrupt their family. All in the pursuit of their happiness which becomes ever more elusive the stranger they get.

So what does all this mean? Pursuit of goals without meaning can be a very frustrating exercise indeed. The good news is that there *is* meaning to your life, but that meaning is not going to come up and announce itself to you. The meaning of your life is something you will need to investigate and discover on your own. Unfortunately, how you discover this meaning is simply something that is not discussed openly or taught in schools. Once you discover meaning, however, the goals become much clearer and start to make sense. Where a goal is an instant frozen in time, meaning and purpose in life are with you 24 hours a day, seven days a week.

Furthermore, you may find it difficult to become truly successful until you do discover the purpose in your life. I am often asked to define success. Success is actively pursuing your purpose in life. You can have all of the money in the world and still not be happy or successful. The converse is also true. I believe it is possible to be penniless and still be a great success. A vivid example of this is Mother Teresa. Early in her life she

Pursuit of goals without meaning can be a very frustrating exercise.

discovered that her purpose was to help those in need. She actively pursued that purpose throughout her life with great energy and vigor. She helped tens of thousands of people in dozens of countries, was world-renowned, won a Nobel Peace Prize, and was obviously an extremely successful individual. Yet, through most of her life she slept on a dirt floor and was penniless.

Some people discover that their purpose in life is to learn. There are thousands of researchers quietly yet persistently laboring to discover the cure for cancer. Many of them do not get paid very high salaries, yet they are, by my definition, extremely successful individuals. They are actively pursuing their purpose in life.

You may wish to ask yourself why you are setting these business goals. What brought you to the job or profession you are currently engaged in? And does that profession fit in with your purpose in life? Many of the conferences and conventions at which I speak are for salespeople. Some of the salespeople I encounter really believe in their products and services, and they work very hard because they believe that by selling more they are truly helping their clients. They are the true successes in business.

If you do not know what your purpose in life is, there are some things you can do to help discover it. First, recognize that purpose does not come knocking at your door. You are not likely to awaken some morning and suddenly just know why you were put here. It does require an active and ongoing effort on your part.

The following is a simple technique that will help you get started on your journey. Sit down and make about a dozen little signs that say, *What am I thinking now?* Post these little signs throughout your home and office where you are likely to see them frequently throughout the day. Perhaps stick them near the telephone, on the copy machine, on your desk drawer, on the door of the refrigerator, on the bathroom mirror, and on the TV stand. For the next few days, whenever you notice one of those little signs, stop and ask yourself, "What was I just thinking?" As you do that, you will begin to recognize that there is always something going on in your subconscious mind.

We often behave as if we have two separate parts of us: the conscious and the subconscious mind. You could be in the most important business meeting of your life, and in the back of your mind be wondering what you are going to have for dinner. You could be fully engaged in a conversation with someone while your subconscious mind is off on a totally different train of thought. In order to discover your purpose you first must understand the patterns of your subconscious mind, and there are going to be patterns. The patterns of your inner thoughts almost always give clues as to the meaning and direction of your life. As you become more and more aware of these patterns, you will begin to recognize what makes you truly happy and purposeful.

> **Purpose does not come knocking at your door.**

For example, one man put the signs up and reported to me that he found himself constantly worried about things. He said that on his way to an appointment, he would look down at his dashboard and see one of the signs and realize that he was worrying that the client might not show up for the appointment. While he was in the appointment, he opened his briefcase, saw one of the signs that he had taped inside the briefcase, and caught himself worrying that the client wasn't going to sign the contract. The client did indeed sign the contract, but a little later as the man was driving home he looked at the dashboard again, saw one of the signs, and caught himself worrying that the client was going to change his mind. He said he really became concerned after he found himself sitting at the kitchen table worrying because he didn't have anything to worry about.

A woman once reported to me that after she put a number of signs up around her house she began noticing that she was always mentally putting herself down. She was constantly second-guessing herself and being self-critical instead of honestly and accurately evaluating her true performance.

Another man told me that when he put up the signs, he noticed that every time he asked himself "What am I thinking?" it turned out to be a negative thought. His wife had been telling him for years that his attitude was negative, but he never believed it until he put up those signs and discovered it for himself.

The previous examples all seem to be quite negative in nature. Hopefully, when you do your analysis, you will have a completely different experience. For example, when you ask yourself, "What am I thinking?" you might notice that you are thinking about how satisfied you are in your chosen profession, how content and fulfilled you are in your personal relationship, how good you feel physically, or simply what a beautiful day it is. If that inner thinking process is consistently positive and upbeat in nature, you are probably well on your way to understanding the purpose and meaning of your life. If you do not like what you find in your subconscious mind, however, now at least you have three different tools to assist you in your quest.

1. You might want to keep the signs up for 21 days. As you notice yourself thinking a positive thought, give yourself some kind of tangible reward; punish yourself if you notice negative or counterproductive thoughts (thus using the kinesthetic approach).

2. You might wish to make a tape to help reprogram your subconscious thinking process for positive and motivating thoughts (the auditory approach).

3. And of course, you could practice self-hypnosis and use the visualization process to help change your inner thinking.

As the inner thinking changes, your outward perspective also begins to alter. And of course, vice-versa. When I was in private psychology practice in Florida, a woman came to me and reported that she had a very good job, was making great money, lived in a fine house, and had all of the material amenities that she wanted, but was

As your inner thinking changes, your outward perspective also begins to alter.

simply not very happy. I asked her what she thought would make her happy, and she said she had always dreamed of living in the mountains in Colorado. She didn't know exactly why she thought this would make her happy, but she always felt that this was where she belonged. My response was, "Why not move out to Colorado and be happy?" She replied that she was lucky to have the job she had, and was making more money than she thought she could make anywhere else. She didn't want to give up the job for fear of losing the really good salary. My advice to her was to put up some *What am I thinking now?* signs and do an inner search. When she came in for her next session, she reported that she had made up her mind: she was moving to Colorado. Every time she saw one of the signs, she noticed that she was wishing she was someplace else. She felt that life was just too short to be spending her time doing something that did not make her feel happy or fulfilled.

I received a couple of postcards from this woman, thanking me for helping her to make what was ultimately the right decision for her. For whatever reason, Colorado was where she belonged, and making the move was what made her truly happy. With a little introspection and serious thought, you too can discover what makes you truly happy, and thus come closer to discovering true purpose and meaning in your life. The goals that you set will then make sense within the larger context of your life.

11

Use These Techniques to Stop Smoking

Just as you can train yourself to create your daily goals for business, you can also use self-hypnosis to program your mind in areas of non-business activities and behaviors. The techniques described in this book can help you stop smoking permanently. But, in order to do so, you should have a good understanding of what the smoking habit is about, how you formed it, and how it is maintained. Armed with this information, you have the ammunition you need to get to work and teach yourself to systematically eliminate this habit for good.

I genuinely feel sorry for a lot of people who are smokers in this culture, because as they were growing up smoking was considered to be rather fashionable and was not stigmatized as it is today. In many respects, the act of smoking used to be glorified. In the movies and in television advertisements — the very same commercials that were subconsciously drummed into your head so effectively over the years — the macho people, the heroes, and the glamorous women were often smokers. The smokers were portrayed as people who were in control of whatever situation they found themselves in. And, of course, today we know that the exact reverse is true. In fact, when people try to stop smoking and are unable to, they are not in control at all.

The bombardment of advertising was, in many ways, responsible for people's smoking habits. As recently as 20 years ago, newspaper, radio, and television ads were heavily laden with cigarette commercials. This repetitious —hypnotic, if you will—commercial advertisement tended to form certain patterns in most people's minds.

Your environment often has a lot to do with whether you are a smoker or not. People who are in high-stress environments will tend to pick up the smoking habit or have more difficulty stopping smoking than people who are in more relaxed environments. When you grew up, if your parents were smokers, statistically speaking you stand a far greater chance of being a smoker as an adult than if your parents were not smokers.

Now I am going show you a way to stop smoking that is a little different than what most people recommend. Most people advocate the "cold turkey" approach to stopping smoking: namely, you pick a day or date, you stop smoking, and you reinforce the habit of not smoking and simultaneously withdraw from nicotine all on that given day. If you are a smoker and have ever tried to stop, you've probably tried this method. In fact, there is even the "Great American Smoke Out" every year, which is a day all the smokers in the country try to stop cold turkey.

Your environment often has a lot to do with whether you are a smoker or not.

But how many of them are right back smoking again a few months later? Or even in a few weeks or days?

I recommend, based on my own personal experience, that you use a gradual withdrawal approach for a variety of very good reasons. However, I forewarn you that statistically speaking the cold turkey approach tends to have a higher success rate than does a gradual reduction. Even though the statistics show a better success rate for the cold turkey approach, I am advising a gradual reduction technique. I am going to explain why the method that is a little bit different could be the one you can finally find success with.

As I mentioned before, hypnosis is going to be involved, which is a bit more unconventional than your standard approaches. But if you think about it, smoking is a habit that is programmed into your brain the way any other habit (bad or good!) is. So it follows that retraining your brain to break the smoking habit would work in a manner similar to the way it does when you retrain your brain to ask for referrals or regularly follow up with clients.

Think about the smoking habit. People tend to smoke for different reasons in the morning than they do in the afternoon or they do in the evening. People smoke for different reasons when they are bored than when they are tired or when they are frustrated. Stopping smoking is a series of little habits and should be approached as such. This is often the problem with the cold turkey approach: it treats smoking as one big habit. If you try to stop smoking all at once, you may be trying to stop 20 small habits simultaneously. You may succeed in battling or repressing

19 of those 20 habits, but if you fall prey to and reignite just one of those little habits, the entire problem may re-emerge. You may go into a bar and see people smoking and drinking; the lure to light up may over-whelm you. Your brain still remembers how smoking while drinking a cold beer was one of your favorite smoking habits. If you are in a bar and you see people lighting up, no matter how successful you have been in quelling the urge to smoke, you can't resist "just this once." Before you know it, you are back to a pack a day. That experience is called "spontaneous recovery." The whole habit comes back: not just when you are in a bar, but for all the other times your brain is used to having nicotine.

> **You can learn to stop smoking systematically, setting the proper conditions.**

You can learn to stop smoking systematically, setting the proper conditions. If you were to reduce the amount you are currently smoking by one half — a goal most people are able to do immediately — you will feel like you have accomplished at least part of your goal, rather than feeling frustrated in the cold turkey approach when you go from your full smoking habit to nothing with no transi-tion period. You start out being successful as opposed to having all that frustration, and your system is not shocked as much with the gradual approach. In fact, as you wean yourself of your habit, you will find that the weakest of the many little habits will start dropping out rather rapidly.

Most of you would agree that, with a concerted effort, you could reduce the amount that you smoke by at least 50 percent. This is because at least half of your smoking habit is totally unconscious. You see someone smoking a cigarette, so you pick one up and you smoke, or you get into a car and you automatically pick up a cigarette. The phone rings, you pick up a cigarette. A lot of this is unconscious behavior, and many chronic smokers have had the experience of lighting a cigarette only to look down in the ashtray and see that there is a cigarette sitting there that is already lit. They were totally unaware as they went about the rather complex act of lighting a cigarette. When you think about smoking, it really is a complex act. That person had to first register in their mind that they had a desire to smoke. Then they had to locate the cigarette pack, take it out of their pocket or purse, pull a cigarette out of the pack, put it in their mouth, light a match, bring the match to the cigarette, light the cigarette, blow out the match, then put the cigarette down. And they completely forget that they had just done all of this. See what I mean? Smoking is not one habit, but a series of many little habits.

It would probably take an experienced trainer years to teach a monkey to perform these same behaviors that smokers do totally unconsciously. So step #1 is to learn to use the self-hypnosis techniques to help you gain control of your smoking. Once you start that process, you will start to notice some physical effects, as well as the psychological ones that come with learning to train your mind to have new habits. Smoking is not only a psychological habit; it is also a physiological habit. People do become addicted, literally, to nicotine. And most people really don't understand what nicotine is or what it does. Nicotine imitates acetyl choline in your central nervous system.

Acetyl choline, or ACH, is one of the five or six primary neurotransmitters that you have in your brain. Neuro-transmitters are chemicals that facilitate the firing of nerve cells.

The nervous system is built on levels of mutual inhi-bition — meaning there are always opposing forces at work in the nervous system. For example, when you go to sleep at night, you are not turning something off, even though it seems like it. Actually, the exact opposite is occurring when you go to sleep. You are very much turn-ing something on. The fact is that when you are awake and alert you are activating a certain nervous system in your body. And a certain neurotransmitter is responsible for activating that nervous system. When you go to sleep, you start activating a different nervous system, and the nervous system that allows you to be awake and alert starts becoming less active, or repressed. Then when you wake up, the "awake" system fires again and the sleep system starts becoming inhibited or repressed.

This exact same process is occurring in smoking. When you smoke a cigarette, your central nervous system is being activated by the ACH chemical I referred to earlier. What people don't realize is that when they are firing this ACH system, they are actually adding a chemical to their bloodstream that their body already produces. Nicotine imitates this naturally occurring chemical and it acts just like acetyl choline in the central nervous system. This in turn raises the relative levels of ACH in that person's body.

Our bodies are pretty smart and compensate for this high level of ACH. Your body is used to having a relative balance of ACH and norepinephrine. You have added more ACH, so your body starts overproducing norepinephrine to try to get back into that relative balance. When people stop smoking what is really occurring, in terms of physiological side effects, is they are no longer getting that extra ACH. Over the years their body has gotten used to it—their body has become addicted to it. That's what addiction is: when your body craves something it is used to getting on a regular basis. So when the addicted body is no longer getting that additional ACH, it is still overproducing norepinephrine. Paradoxically, the physical effects of stopping smoking are more a matter of your body continuing to crave this one chemical as opposed to withdrawing from nicotine. What a person should feel physiologically are symptoms such as a runny nose, watery eyes, or a sluggish feeling. But that is not always the case.

When they stop smoking, people have physical symptoms that run the whole gamut. If you have ever tried to stop, you don't need me to tell you this. Some people get nervous, some people start eating, some people feel jittery. So it is the matter of that relative balance. When you gradually withdraw, you overcome the problem of shocking your whole system. You literally teach your body, as well as your mind, to adjust to new levels of behavior and, in the body's case, new levels of this chemical.

Another important adjustment that you make as a nonsmoker is social. To go from being a smoking person to a nonsmoking person can have some fairly dramatic effects on your social life. If you habitually go into a restaurant and ask for the smoking section, or you are

Becoming a nonsmoking person can have some pretty dramatic effects on your social life.

used to hanging out with colleagues in the smoking lounge, you are going to be adjusting to a new self-image. As part of your gradual withdrawal, why not go into your favorite restaurant and, for once, request a seat in the nonsmoking section, just to see if you can do it? This is just one of the series of little habits which make up your larger smoking habit. If you conquer one at a time, little step by little step, it isn't all that bad, is it?

Take a look at what is one of the most powerful of all the little habits that most smokers encounter: the after-meal cigarette. A lot of people have a hard time finishing a meal without lighting up a cigarette. But if you approach it as a series of little habits, the after-meal cigarette is actually only a three-cigarette-a-day habit. If you approach it as such, stopping is not an insurmountable goal. If you work just on that three-cigarette-a-day habit for a day or two, you would probably find you could lick that fairly easily. But if you are trying to battle that three-cigarette-a-day habit while you are also battling the smoking and drinking habit, or while you are also battling the smoking and being frustrated, nervous, or on the phone habit, all together this could overload your nervous system. And it can overload your mind. If you gradually reduce day by day, you decrease the amount you smoke and help your body and mind adjust to the new reality.

Stopping smoking cold turkey is similar in many respects to people who go on a crash diet. Personally, I don't believe that people who are dieting are learning anything. For them to wake up in the morning and say, "All right, as of this morning I am not going to eat ice cream or cake, and I am not going to behave in the way I have been behaving for the past ten years of my life," is unrealistic play-acting. They are not learning anything. They get on a diet and shrink down, however much they are going to lose. Then they go right back to their old way and their old style of eating. The same thing often occurs when people take the cold turkey approach to stopping smoking. "All right, as of today, I am going to act like I am a nonsmoker." But they are not really learning to be a nonsmoker at all.

Notice the choice of words I have made. I am not talking about a person who has *quit* smoking; I am talking about a person who has *stopped* smoking. There is a very big difference. People who are quitting smoking are implying that they are giving something up.

Over the years I've asked people who were attempting to stop smoking: "What do you suppose would happen if you were to stop smoking this very instant? Let's wave a magic wand over your head and all of the sudden that urge to smoke is totally and completely gone. You are a nonsmoker. What is going to happen to you in your life?"

Of the people I have asked, there tends to be a 50-50 split. Half of the people typically say, "I would feel so good. I would be so happy. The fear of cancer would be gone. I would be so proud of myself. I wouldn't smell lousy anymore." Now, those of you who are thinking along those lines stand a very good chance of succeeding with this program.

The other half of the people who claim they want to stop smoking answer, "I'd gain 15 pounds. I'd be a nervous wreck. I'd climb the walls." If this is the way you are thinking, you are going to have a serious problem. You had better re-evaluate your reasons for stopping smoking. Why do you really want to stop? Most people will say they don't want to get cancer, they don't want to be ill, and they don't want to die from emphysema. But that doesn't stop people from smoking, obviously.

I've worked with hundreds and hundreds of people to help them stop smoking. I've worked with people who have had tracheotomies, lungs removed, emphysema, and who have been on their deathbeds smoking cigarettes. One man was wheeled into the operating room to have a lung removed. I was there, trying to help him with self-hypnosis, and he had to have just one more cigarette before he had that operation. So fear of death is really not going to stop you. The things that are meaningful are! If you are trying to stop smoking because your spouse or your friends are bugging you to stop smoking, forget it—you are going to have a real uphill battle. But if you stop because of your own self-image, because of the way you see yourself in relation to the world around you, because *you* want to, you stand a very good chance of becoming a permanent nonsmoker.

Some people realize that their smoking habit has been programmed into their brain since they were a youngster, and in many cases the way it happened was quite beyond their control. Now here they are with this idea locked into their subconscious mind since childhood, and as adults they are trying to stop smoking, because as adults they see themselves as being a different kind of person. They come to the realization that smoking is just not the way they want to be. These people stand an excellent chance of becoming permanent nonsmokers. And there are some very simple things you can do to help yourself stop smoking.

When you think about how you started smoking, you are looking at a powerful form of hypnosis. Over and over and over in your life it was suggested to you that smoking was a good thing to do. It was suggested to you through the media that smoking was suave, that smoking was sexy, that smoking was glamorous and sophisticated. Now notice what occurred with the first cigarette you took. Your body said, "No, no, no. Please don't do this to me." You took that first puff and, if you were the average person, you coughed, you sputtered, your head started spinning, and perhaps you felt downright nauseous.

But look at what you did to learn how to smoke. You forced your body to adhere to your conscious wishes. Maybe you wanted to start because you thought you would look like an adult, or to rebel against your parents, or because everyone else was doing it, or because you were just plain hypnotized by advertisements. You really wanted to start smoking and, through repetition, you had a lot of information to learn.

For example, you had to learn how to hold the cigarette, how not to put three-quarters of it in your mouth at one time, when were times that you could and could not smoke, and how to inhale. Some people even learned how to blow smoke rings, how to blow the smoke back up their nose in a French inhale. The point is you had a *lot* of stuff to learn in order to become a smoker. So it makes sense that in order to become a nonsmoker, the same is true: you have a lot to learn—or unlearn. Using the same systematic repetition you used to put that negative information in there, we're going to put positive information in there.

Modify Your Smoking Habit

A second technique is a behavior modification technique. Just like you did when writing down your short- and long-term business goals, get a piece of paper and write down every time you have a cigarette:

- What time of day is it?

- What is your mood like when you crave the cigarette?

- What number cigarette is it for the day?

- What position are you in?

- Who are you with?

For the next few days, gather this valuable information about yourself. Every time you reach for that cigarette, have that piece of paper folded up and in the cigarette pack and—if you have enough motivation, and you really want to stop smoking—every time you go to take a cigarette, write down the answers to the above questions. You will find that this will automatically help you reduce your smoking by at least 50 percent. Just becoming conscious of your smoking habits will help you immensely to gain control. When you look over that list and you see "Wow! This is cigarette number seven and the last cigarette I had was 10 o'clock. Here it is 10:15," and you say to yourself that since that was only 15 minutes ago, you don't need another cigarette yet. You will be able to gain control. If you are running down that list and you see that you smoke when you feel bored, you can tell yourself that there are more constructive ways to deal with boredom. Start by drawing your conscious attention to the habit itself, then "reduce and gain": reduce the amount of smoking, and gain control by at least 50 percent.

But more than that, if you keep that list consistently and honestly for the next few days, you are going to receive some valuable information about yourself. You keep notes on your business contacts. Why not on yourself? You will begin to see in black and white what is really maintaining that smoking habit.

I had a client who came to a profound realization from keeping this list. She kept it for four or five days. When she looked at the list, much to her astonishment, under the category of what position she was in, she noticed she was always sitting down. Somewhere along the line, she had learned not to smoke while standing up. She remembered that her mother had once told her it was very unladylike to smoke while standing up, so she had a subconscious habit programmed along with the smoking habit: whenever she had to stand up while she had a lit cigarette, she would leave the cigarette in the ashtray. When she came back she would sit down and finish smoking it. This woman really wanted to stop smoking, so the simplest thing for her to do to help control her habit was whenever she got the urge to smoke, stand up! She found this simple behavior really helped.

Pay close attention to the situations you put yourself in when you smoke.

If you hang out with a bunch of smokers, you are probably going to be a smoker. Not that you should avoid or stigmatize people just because they have the smoking habit. I'm not saying that at all. But at least initially while you are learning to stop smoking, avoid situations that you know for a fact will precipitate the smoking habit. It would be wise to stay out of bars for a few days if you know that the smoking-and-drinking combination is a powerful habit for you. If you like to sit down at the end of an evening meal and puff away on your cigarette, make it a point to get up from the table as soon as you finish eating and perhaps start doing the dishes right away. For the next few days, if you know you have the choice of going to see two friends, one a chronic smoker and the other a nonsmoker, do yourself a favor and spend time with the one who is not a smoker. And continually think of yourself as a person who is not a smoker.

If you are not sufficiently motivated by the huge amount of information available on the health risks of smoking, maybe an economic approach will help you put a stop to your smoking habit. Last time I looked, cigarettes cost about $3 a pack. If you are a two-pack-a-day smoker that's $6 a day. Over the course of a year we are talking about more than $2,000! That's a lot of money. But that's not enough for most people to stop smoking. You can tell someone they would save thousand of dollars in a year's time by stopping smoking cigarettes, but that alone usually doesn't motivate people sufficiently.

Remember how any event followed by a pleasurable experience is likely to be repeated, while any event followed by a punishment will very likely be avoided? That principle holds true here too. If you really want to help yourself stop smoking, set a small personal goal for yourself. As you reduce your smoking, make an agreement with yourself. For every day you stay on schedule with your gradual-reduction technique, give yourself a little reward. It could be ten minutes of free time, a new magazine, or a piece of jewelry. And for every day that you do not succeed in reaching your goal—if you smoke 25 cigarettes, instead of the 20 that you promised yourself—produce a little self-punishment. I am not talking about flailing yourself on the back with a whip, but maybe make yourself go to bed an hour later than usual (or an hour earlier, whichever is a "punishment" for you). Perhaps don't allow yourself to watch a favorite television program. Maybe make yourself do a little chore around the house that you ordinarily wouldn't have done. Set a series of punishments as well as a series of rewards; you'll find that this technique really does work.

While you are moving toward becoming a nonsmoker, your mental image—the way you think about yourself—is going to start to change. And, of course, as you stop smoking, you are going to feel a lot better. Even if you smoked for 10, 15, or 20 years, the human body has tremendous recuperative powers. Your body can recover in as little as two weeks and eliminate over 90 percent of all the garbage you have been throwing down your lungs all those years. Now I am not going to lie to you and tell you your lungs are going to be pink and clean like they were never damaged. But your body's restorative powers are going to eliminate a lot of those toxins, and your chances of getting cancer are going to be vastly reduced. Even in the precancerous condition, before people cross that mysterious line into producing cancer cells, the body is often able to defend itself, and recuperate almost 100 percent.

If you stop smoking, you will look better, you'll feel better, you'll save money, you'll be happier, you'll be more successful. And let's face it—this place is rapidly becoming a nonsmoking world. Join the "in" crowd. Enjoy your life!

Affirmations for Stopping Smoking

The following is a list of suggestions and affirmations you may wish to give to yourself while in the hypnotic state.

1. I am a nonsmoker.

2. I enjoy the benefits of not smoking.

3. Not smoking is pleasurable.

4. I am in complete control of the smoking habit at all times.

5. I enjoy breathing easier.

6. Fresh-smelling clothes are pleasurable to me.

7. I enjoy more energy and vitality as a nonsmoker.

8. I am glad to be setting a positive role model for future generations.

12

Learn to Control Your Weight Forever

If you can alter your business performance or your smoking habits, then it follows that you can use the power of your self-image to teach yourself to lose weight and keep it off permanently.

I will start by telling you right up front that the only way you will ever permanently lose weight is to permanently change your style of eating. It requires a systematic series of steps whereby you change your preference for foods and your style of eating. A while ago, a health organization commissioned a study of obesity in American males and females. The man who headed this study was one of the foremost researchers on the subject of obesity. He published his report after years of intensive study, and the conclusions were rather dismal. It found that most obese people do not seek treatment for obesity. Most people who *do* seek treatment for obesity drop out of that treatment. And most people who lose weight — whether or not they are obese — gain it all back again. These discouraging facts are what the experts have to say about weight loss programs.

> ## Most people who lose weight—whether or not they are obese—gain it all back again.

Statistically speaking (see how statistics keep sneaking in here?) weight loss has the highest recidivism rate of any habit—worse than smoking, and worse than alcoholism. Losing weight and keeping it off is a national problem. Obviously, drastic steps are needed to control the problem permanently.

I am not telling you this to frighten or discourage you. I am trying to be honest with you: losing weight permanently is going to take some real commitment on your part. There really are no easy solutions. Unfortunately, in our Western culture, food tends to be a big part of our lives. You walk into someone's house and the first thing they usually do is offer you cookies or cake or something to drink. If you refuse their offer, you may feel like you are offending your host. Every time you watch television, there are all kinds of food commercials (commercials again are one of the culprits!) that literally make your mouth water when you watch them. Everywhere we turn, there are all kinds of advertisements and subliminal cues trying to get us to eat.

To control your eating habits permanently first requires that you develop a new self-image and perception of yourself. I have been talking about self-image throughout the book, so the concept is now familiar. Think about how you picture yourself. Be honest with yourself. The picture you just pulled out of your subconscious mind is a fairly good representation of what you think you are supposed to look like in relation to the world around you. If you just unconsciously pulled out a picture of an overweight person, you are going to have a weight problem until you change that picture. And it doesn't matter what diet you get on. You can get on the world's greatest diet and lose 50, 60, 100 pounds, but if every time you stop and think about yourself, you're seeing a picture of an overweight person, you will rapidly go back to looking the way you think you are supposed to look.

You may be asking yourself, "How do I know if I have a self-image problem? What if I have gotten so used to the mental image I keep that I cannot tell if it is accurate or not?" Well, here is one big clue as to whether your problem is with image or not. People who have an image problem probably have at least two sets of clothes. They've got their "fat" clothes and their "skinny" clothes. They diet and they yo-yo, but they hold onto their over-weight clothes, even though they lose weight. They keep those fat clothes because they know and they keep telling themselves, "Sooner or later I'll be back there again." And sure enough, most of them are.

Let's look for a moment at what a diet is. Just like smokers fool themselves into thinking they will stop smoking cold turkey, most people who diet do exactly the same thing. They decide: "Starting tomorrow at 8 o'clock, I'm going on a diet and I'm not going to eat ice cream and I'm not going to eat between meals and I'm not going to eat candy." This is a big joke. It is a play-acting routine, because as soon as they get off the diet, they go right back to the old eating style that caused the problem in the first place. If you are going to permanently lose weight, you must permanently change your way of looking at food.

There are a series of remarkably simple things you can do that result in permanent weight loss over time. Let me give you one example. If you were simply to chew your food twice as long as you're currently chewing it (i.e., double the amount of time you are chewing your food), most of you would lose seven pounds over the course of a year just from the extra calories you were burning up with your jaw movement. Conversely, if you kept your style of eating exactly the way it is right now, and all you did was add one little piece of chocolate layer cake every day, you would gain over 20 pounds in a year from the calories in that chocolate layer cake. Maintaining your weight is a very simple equation. It is

> **To permanently lose weight, you must change your way of looking at food.**

the number of calories that go into your body in relation to the number of calories you burn up. Whatever calories are left over tend to get stored in your body in the form of adipose or fat. So when we look at the weight equation, we are going to look at both sides of that equation: the number of calories that are coming into your body as well as the number of calories you are utilizing or burning up.

Let's look at the latter question first: the number of calories you are burning up. Take a look at your activity level. The average American spends 49.6 hours a week watching television. And you don't see too many people watching television and jogging at the same time. So let's look at your activity level and how to increase it. There are some very simple things to do. If you really want to lose weight, get in the habit of parking your car just a little bit farther away from the store. Some people waste gallons of gas driving a 3,000-pound automobile around, looking for a parking space close to front door. They would be doing themselves and the economy a favor if they parked their car down at the end of the lot and walked a few extra yards to the store.

Here's another idea. When you walk into a building and you have to go up to the fifth floor, every now and then at least, why not take the stairs instead of standing there waiting for the elevator? If you can get into the habit of doing simple little things like this, you will feel better, you will look better, and you will lose a lot of weight.

What I am going to show you next is a technique for measuring output that is very simple and effective. The first step is to purchase a pedometer. A pedometer is one of those little gadgets that you stick in your pocket or clip on one of your shoes and it tells you how far you have walked. There are at least two kinds of pedometers, one for jogging and one for walking. Make sure you buy the walking pedometer. Purchase this pedometer and stick it underneath your belt, in your pocket, or underneath your pants cuff, and monitor your activity level for just a couple of days. This is what we call "gathering baseline data." Monitor your daily activity and you may be surprised at how little you actually walk.

During a few days of average activity, you come back each day and write down on a piece of paper what the pedometer tells you. Perhaps you discover after three days that you are walking a mile a day. Now you have some very valuable information. All you have to do is keep that pedometer with you for the next couple of weeks, and make it a personal goal to increase the amount that you are walking just a little bit each day. Please don't go crazy with this technique. Don't try and go immediately from one mile a day to five miles a day. This would be too much of a shock for your body, and you won't want to walk that far ever again. Remember, as with stopping smoking and other habits that need to be programmed, *gradual* behavior modification is the best way to be successful.

If you keep that pedometer you'll be very aware that it is on your body. This will help focus your conscious attention on activity, and you will find the motivation to take the stairs instead of the elevator or park the car a little farther away. It's really remarkable, when people turn their attention to a given behavior, just how much control they can exert through a conscious, aware state of mind. This focusing of attention can assist with the process of inhibition. So increase your activity level with the use of a pedometer. Don't go wild with it, but just keep it on your body and you'll get some very valuable information.

Here's another simple trick that will increase the length of time that you chew your food and result in weight loss over a period of time. Don't put any food on your fork or spoon until you have swallowed what's in your mouth. Overweight people tend to have a consistent eating pattern. If you ever watch a person who really gets into food, they'll take a mouthful of food and, while they still have that food in their mouth, they'll load up the fork or

> **It's really remarkable how much control we can exert through a conscious, aware state of mind.**

the spoon. They will be sitting there looking at the food they are about to eat, not paying any attention at all to the food they are already eating. This causes them to speed up their eating process. If you have two people, one of whom is eating quickly while the other is eating slowly, it is highly predictable which person will consume more food, because of something called the glucostat mechanism. This mechanism causes a time lag between the moment your stomach is full and the moment it registers in your hypothalamus that you feel full. If you are eating rapidly, your stomach may actually be full ten minutes before you start feeling full. In that ten minutes, a rapid eater can consume a lot more food. Anything you can do to slow your eating down will help you feel full with less food.

Another technique is to use a smaller plate. Some people have these gigantic plates. They may look nice on a formal table, but people forget about surface area. You remember from high school geometry that the area of a circle is πr^2 where r is the radius of the circle. If you are eating on a four-inch plate, the radius is 2×2 (2 squared), or 4. Look what happens when you eat from a six-inch plate. The radius is now 3×3 (3 squared), or 9. *This is more than twice the surface area of the four-inch plate,* even though a four-inch plate doesn't look much bigger than a six-inch plate. Many overeaters are unconsciously conditioned to the sight of a full plate of food. Most people are surprised to find that, with a smaller plate, they still get the subconscious experience of eating a full plate of food. But in the end they eat much less.

Here's another tip for losing weight permanently. Learn to eat in one place and one place only. Pick a spot in the house where you are going to eat. If you are eating in more than one room in the house, you are eating in a dissociated fashion. You are literally not paying attention to what's going on. And when you become dissociated, you lose control. An example of dissociation is a person who sits in front of a TV set, gets absorbed in a movie or a program, and starts munching away on potato chips. They automatically reach down and they are eating these potato chips as they get more and more absorbed in the movie. As they reach down for the umpteenth time, the bag is empty. And of course their response is: "I can't believe I ate the whole thing." One part of them was not paying attention to what the other part was doing.

If you take that same person and that same bag of potato chips, pour the potato chips on a plate, and then hand them that mountain of potato chips on the plate and say, "Here, I want you to sit down and eat these," most people could not get even a third of the way through before they would feel satisfied. But if one part of you is watching a television program and another part is putting the potato chips in your mouth, and you're not paying attention to the cues your body is sending you, you can consume an enormous amount of food. So force yourself to pay attention to what you are doing. That will give you more control.

Another tip is to never eat out of a box or a bag. Always put your food on a plate (preferably a small plate). Once again, you could sit and wolf down a dozen Oreos and not pay attention. But if you see 12 Oreos piled up on a plate, and you sit down to eat all of them, it makes a big psychological difference. While you are practicing these simple techniques, you'll find that over a period of time they really do make a big difference in how many calories you actually consume.

If you just read the chapter on stopping smoking, you will notice that the principles for quitting smoking and modifying eating habits are very similar. Both require taking little steps that eventually add up to you conquering a negative eating or smoking habit.

Many people find that these simple techniques of behavior modification are beneficial because they reveal their eating habits and help them focus on the real problem. For this next technique, get a piece of paper and draw vertical lines on it to create five columns or categories.

- Category 1 is time of day.
- Category 2 is what position you are in.
- Category 3 is who you are with.
- Category 4 is what your mood is.
- Category 5 is where you are.

Keep this piece of paper with you at all times. Any time during the day that you go to eat something, take it out and mark down the information in each category.

Once you have kept this chart for two or three weeks, sit down and analyze it. The beauty of this chart is that it helps in at least two ways. First, you'll gain control of your eating behavior just by monitoring it. Monitoring an unconscious behavior almost always reduces it. Many people are very surprised to discover that they completely control their eating habits as long as they are monitoring them.

Second, and perhaps more valuable, is that if you are honest with yourself, if you really monitor the time of day, what position you are in, who you are with and the like, you will start to see the patterns of your eating behavior. Of course, the data is never completely clear-cut. But it does form patterns. Some people learn that they are eating every hour, so the best way to get control of their eating is to concentrate on increasing the time between eating. Others find that they eat in a certain position. Perhaps they tend to snack whenever they are sitting in a certain chair or lying in a certain position. The obvious solution to that particular pattern is to sit in a different chair or assume a different position when they feel the urge to eat. Some people discover that there are certain people who trigger their eating. They may always eat with their spouse or their children or with a friend across the street. If they really want to lose weight, they may choose to avoid that person or consciously try to control themselves while they are with that person.

Many people with weight problems discover that the mood they are most often in when they eat is feeling guilty. I would like to point out something about guilt. I believe that the source of all human guilt is people trying to lie to themselves. Some people, especially those with unhealthy eating habits, go on binges where they overeat and then feel very guilty afterwards. Or people with eating problems will look at a piece of cake and tell themselves, "I will have that one piece of cake, but I promise myself I won't have dessert tomorrow." And then they eat the cake. If they know that they are honestly going to discipline themselves and skip the cake tomorrow, there is no guilt

> **Learning to control your eating habits can be almost fun as you begin to understand the underlying motivation for your actions.**

involved. They just have a little contract with themselves. But if, at the end of eating that piece of cake they feel guilty, the reason they feel this is probably because they know that they are not going to skip dessert the next night. The source of guilt is almost always trying to tell yourself a lie. Keep this in mind when you are keeping those charts, and do your best to be honest with yourself.

When you are analyzing your charts to discover the real motivations behind your eating, patterns tend to emerge. Learning to control your eating habits can be almost fun as you begin to understand the underlying motivation for your actions.

It is a sad but true fact, for many people who have weight problems, that if they cared more about their own wants and needs and less about the wants and needs of others, they wouldn't have a weight problem. Typically those people who overeat do so out of frustration. And typically the really overweight person is genuinely a very nice person. You'll often see these people are everybody's friend. People think they can drop into their house any time they want. Acquaintances are always asking them for favors. And that person is more than happy to oblige. But they also often feel underappreciated and frustrated because they are unable to assert themselves. Part of the process of beating a chronic weight problem is for them to learn to assert themselves.

Part of the process of beating a chronic weight problem is for people to assert themselves.

Saying no to food can be a real problem for these people. There are a couple of simple techniques that work well. You walk into someone's house and they ask you, "Would you like a piece of cake?" or "Can I get you something to eat?" You say "No." And they say, "But I made this chocolate cake just for you. I know you love chocolate cake. Go ahead and have a piece." And you say, "No, thank you." If you say no, you may feel as though you are offending them. If you say, "I'm trying to lose weight," you risk opening yourself up to sabotage.

Here's an alternative. If the person asks, "Would like a piece of cake?" and you say no, and they ask you again, answer: "What I would really like is a glass of ice water," or "What I would really like is some lemonade." Now you have given your host the opportunity to fulfill your needs. If that person offered you something because they truly want to serve you something you want, and you give them the opportunity to serve you a glass of ice water, they have now completely fulfilled their social obligations.

When you are out at a restaurant, you may also need to assert yourself. This can be done in a variety of simple ways. If you know that you are a sucker for bread and rolls, you can request that your server bring just one serving to you, not the whole basket. If you order a piece of grilled fish, you might request that your server make sure it is prepared with no butter or grease.

It helps to understand the value of calories as well.

Some people are absolute computers when it comes to how many calories are in an item of food. Some have memorized calorie counts all the way down the line. If that's the case, utilize this information. Make a little chart for yourself. Think of yourself as "spending calories." If you are following a 1,500- or a 1,300-calorie-a-day diet, imagine that the calories are in a bank account. If you have 150 or 250 calories for breakfast, imagine that you are deducting that from your bank account. If you have 500 calories at lunch, imagine you've withdrawn that number of calories. Then you can spend the rest of your calories later in the evening. Think of calories as a little savings account and try, just as you would save your money, to save on those calories a little bit each day. This is a great way for people who are experts on calories to put that information to good use.

What I have outlined here are a variety of different techniques. Any one of them will result in weight loss over a period of time.

> **Any one of these techniques will result in weight loss over a period of time.**

It is important that you recognize we are dealing with changing habits over a longer span of time. Quick weight loss programs almost never work permanently. Follow these suggestions, and within two weeks you will notice a difference. As you do notice this difference, you will be developing a new style of eating and changing your attitudes about yourself and the world around you. You will look and feel better, and you will probably be delighted to discover that people will treat you better when you control your eating habits.

Affirmations for Weight Control

The following are some affirmations and suggestions for permanently controlling your eating habits.

1. I am in complete control of my eating habits at all times.

2. Not eating is pleasurable.

3. When I eat, I prefer low-calorie, healthful foods that are good for me.

4. Every day I am gaining more control over my eating habits.

5. I see myself looking the way I want to look and feeling the way I want to feel.

6. I am feeling stronger and healthier as I gain control over all of my eating habits.

7. Small amounts of food make me feel very satisfied.

8. My body feels more energetic each day.

9. I feel good about myself and my body.

13

Finding a Mentor

Your subconscious mind is strongly influenced by the people you spend time with. In many respects we are a direct reflection of our environment, and we unconsciously draw toward us people who have similar attitudes and ideologies.

There is a simple test you can perform to reveal what kind of attitude you have. Write down on a piece of paper the five people with whom you voluntarily spend the majority of your time. "Voluntarily" is the key word, because, for example, at the workplace you may not be able to control who you spend your time with. Now take a look at that list. It will tell you a lot about yourself.

One middle manager told me that, when he analyzed his list, he discovered that most of his friends had negative outlooks and a series of personal problems that were largely self-induced. One of his friends had a drug problem. Another was involved in an abusive relationship with his spouse. Still another tended to be dishonest. After making the list, he realized that each of these people in their own way was negatively influencing his chances of becoming the person he really wanted to be.

We tend to become like the people with whom we interact. If you don't think that environment influences your attitude, try this experiment. On the way home from work tonight, stop off at your local funeral parlor. If there is a wake in progress, sit in the parlor for five minutes and notice how you feel. Even though you have no idea who the deceased person is, if you spend five minutes surrounded by grief you will probably notice a change in your outlook by the time you leave. Imagine now what spending days on end with a negative person does to your outlook.

If you are not happy with your situation, here is what you can do to change it. First, decide what kind of a person you want to become. What kind of values and attitudes are important to you? Consciously seek out and cultivate friendships and relationships with these kinds of people. Next—and this is the hard part—spend as little time as possible with people who would be a negative influence on you. Sometimes this requires that you give up acquaintances or friendships you have had for years. In fact, you do pay a price for success—and this may be one of those prices.

When I was in graduate school, I had a friend who was starting a career in sales. At the time, we had a number of shared values and mutual friends. After I completed my graduate work, I moved to another locale and fell out of touch with him. About ten years later, I was pleased to discover that he had moved to a few miles from where I was living. I suggested that we meet for dinner and catch up on old times. Unfortunately the last ten years had not gone well for him. His career had never really taken off and he had had a series of personal setbacks. He had been divorced twice, was battling a drug problem, and had a terribly negative attitude about nearly everything. I suggested that he read a few books that had really impacted my thinking, and I encouraged him to take responsibility for his actions and move forward.

A few weeks later, we got together again for dinner. This time he told me that he had just been fired from his job because his boss accused him of stealing. When I asked him if he had followed up on any of my suggestions, he stated that he was just too busy. About a month later, I saw him yet again and still he had done nothing to change.

At that point, I had a decision to make. Every time I met with him was depressing for me. I truly would have liked to have helped him, but he gave absolutely no indication that he wanted my help or that he was willing to do anything I suggested. The values that we had shared in the past did not transfer to the present. My decision was to stop calling him, because if I was going to reach my own goals, I needed to be surrounded by people who had the same aspirations and motivations. He will always be my friend and I will help him in any way I can, but I no longer initiate the contacts. Given a choice, I deliberately choose to spend my time in a more constructive manner.

Recognizing that the people you spend time with influence your behavior and attitude, you should find a mentor to help you along. There is no reason for you to reinvent the wheel. There is no mistake in business that hasn't already been made. So it is not necessary for you to re-make the very same mistakes on your own pathway to

> **Find a mentor to help you along. There is no reason for you to reinvent the wheel.**

success. There are, no doubt, those who have come before you who have already done it wrong or backwards. These people could give you valuable advice on what not to do, as well as show you the better pathway to follow. Having a mentor could save you years of frustration and mediocre performance.

At this point review your long-term goals. Once again, seriously ask yourself how much money you want to be earning, what kind of position you want to be in, and what kind of home you would like to be living in. Then deliberately find someone who is already there and stick to that person like glue. Pick up the phone, call that person, and invite him or her to breakfast or lunch. Explain in advance exactly what you are trying to do. Tell them that you want to be where they already are. And that you would be grateful if they would give you a few minutes of their time so you could ask them for some advice.

In all likelihood, one of two things will happen: they will either accept or politely decline your invitation. If they decline, simply find someone else who will accept your offer. However, you will probably be pleasantly surprised to find that most truly successful people will find time to meet with you. There are two reasons for this. The first is that having someone ask for your advice is a flattering experience, and people basically love to give advice. The second reason is more fundamental. If you remember back to the example of the bell curve, you will notice that the higher you go in terms of income and productivity, the fewer people there are. You've heard the saying, "It's lonely at the top." Indeed, successful people sometimes find it difficult to find others like them, who are willing to spend the time and effort necessary to become a high achiever. When you contact them, they may very well relate to what you are doing, because in all likelihood at one time in their lives they did exactly the same thing.

Prepare in advance for your meeting. Have some very specific questions. Ask your mentor for advice on how to handle any problems that you may be encountering. Now, here is the hard part: Take their advice. Assume in advance that they know more than you do and have the benefit of experience. Do not talk yourself out of some excellent guidance. At the very least, try doing what they suggest for a reasonable period of time. If it does not work for you, at least you will have given it an honest attempt. Often, when presented with sound guidance, people talk themselves out of taking the advice simply because it seems unfamiliar.

I once met a man who was a successful Massachusetts Mutual insurance agent. He told me he enjoyed mentoring agents, and that every agent he had ever mentored was currently earning more than $100,000 a year. Because of this, he frequently received calls from people asking for guidance. He had developed a simple screening test. He told anyone calling him for help that he would be happy to mentor them if they do the following: Every business day, for the next month, they were to set three appointments by phone and keep a chart they could show him at the end of the month. He considers three appointments a day the minimum performance level for a successful insurance agent. He explained that he never heard from most of the people again because they were simply paying "lip service" to becoming a success. But every once in a while, an agent would call him back 30 days later and present him with a completed chart. At that point, he knew he had an agent who would accept his guidance and be willing to put in the effort required to succeed. If your mentor tells you to stand on your head five minutes every morning before you walk out the door, try it! Who knows? It just might work!

There is another effect that often occurs. Many times people have told me that after their first meeting with a successful person, they had the feeling: "If they can do it, so can I!" One person, after spending time with a man worth millions, said he was amazed that this person was able to be a success at all. The point is that, typically, successful people are not smarter, better, or more charismatic than you are. They are successful because they are willing to do what—up until now—you have not done.

Summary

Having personally attended literally dozens of different goal-setting programs, I have come to the conclusion that one aspect of the seminars which is often sorely lacking is a hands-on, practical approach to setting and achieving one's business objectives. I have often heard about the "gold in goals" and how important it is to have a clear-cut focus in your personal as well as business life, but rarely are any concrete techniques presented.

Throughout this book, a serious attempt has been made to give you not one, but actually three completely independent and very effective ways to internalize your objectives. You may ask why three different techniques and not just one. Being a strong believer in the bell curve, it became obvious that any single technique would affect roughly 68 percent of a group in an average way, 15 to 20 percent in a very powerful way, and the other 15 to 20 percent would receive little or no benefit from that particular approach. Some of the clients I have worked with have said they found the self-hypnosis to be difficult for them, but they were already in the habit of listening to motivational and sales tapes while driving in their car. These people found the auditory approach particularly appealing to them. Others reported exactly the opposite.

They said that they could not imagine listening to the sound of their own voice on a tape, but were pleasantly surprised to find that they were excellent hypnotic subjects and responded readily to their own hypnotic suggestions. Still others said that the reward-and-punishment concept made the most sense to them and was easiest to utilize.

It's no surprise that some people respond more readily to one technique than another. This is probably due to the individual differences in the way people process information. One simple way of looking at this is that some people do most of their thinking on a given day in pictures, whereas others do most of their thinking in words. Think about it. You are capable of doing both types of thinking. For example, you could easily think in pictures if you were remembering what your home or one of your loved ones looks like. If you chose to, you could just as easily think in words if you were reciting the Pledge of Allegiance out loud. Even though you can easily do both types of information processing, chances are that you favor one type over the other. People who do most of their thinking in pictures will tend to find the self-hypnosis more effective, whereas those who think in words will find the auditory approach suits them best.

But any of the three techniques in this book will be effective for you if it is utilized properly and consistently. Indeed, many people have reported to me that they have used all three techniques simultaneously to reach their goals. A few have told me they used two of the three concepts simultaneously. However, in all likelihood, you will get better results by choosing one approach and sticking with it to completion. The important thing is that you need to do *something* to create the focus and drive necessary to get to where you want to be. Toward that end, this book should be an invaluable aid.

Supplemental Reading

The Origin of Consciousness in the Breakdown of the Bicameral Mind. Julian Jaynes

Hypnotic Realities. Milton H. Erickson and Ernst Rossi

Suggestion and Auto-Suggestion. Emile Coue

Superlearning. Lynn Schroeder and Sheila Ostrander

Using Both Sides of Your Brain. Tony Buzan

Theories of Learning. E.R. Hilgard and G.H. Bower

Theories of Motivation. R.C. Bolles

"Left Brain/Right Brain." *Saturday Review,* 1975, 2 30–33

How to Get Control of Your Time and Your Life. Alan Lakein

Using Your Brain for a Change. Richard Bandler

Change Your Mind and Keep the Change. Steve and Connirae Andreas

Doors of Perception. Aldous Huxley

Want to learn more?

Anthony Galie offers a complete series of educational audio cassettes and an exciting videotape capturing his hypnotic goal-setting presentation. The audio tapes are divided into three sets as follows:

SET I - Personal Development Series

Self-hypnosis I: Learn self-hypnosis in the comfort of your own home.

Self-hypnosis II: Want to take it to the next step? Here are the more advanced techniques of self-hypnosis.

Stop Smoking: Proven behavior modification technique to help you stop smoking permanently. Hypnotic suggestion included on side B.

Weight Control: Change your eating behavior and lose weight permanently. Hypnotic induction on side B.

Motivation: How to stay motivated over long periods of time.

Deep Relaxation: Learn to relax—hypnotically.

Price: $15 each ■ $79.95/set

SET II - Business Development Series

Attitude: Techniques for developing a positive mental attitude with hypnotic induction for reinforcement.

Creativity: Learn to be more creative in your business and personal life by using the power of your subconscious mind.

Managing Your Time: A most unique approach to time management by learning to focus on the here and now.

Success: Find out what "IT" is all about.

Nonverbal Communication: Learn how a therapist reads their clients' signals and how you can apply the same techniques to your business.

Indirect Suggestion: Learn to communicate with your client's subconscious mind—where the sale is really made.

Price: $15 each ■ $79.95/set

SET III – Tony Galie "Live" Series

A six-pack of live presentations from around the country. These presentations were drawn directly from Tony's seminars and stage appearances and capture the essence of his training program. If you liked the seminar, you'll love the tapes.

- Tony's "four-point presentation" on goal-setting

- Learn how to get your goals on tape using the Baroque Learning System

- Tried-and true-closing strategies

- Listen and learn how to program in winning habits

Price: $79.95

Video Tape – Tony on Video!

Live at the Grand Ole Opry in front of an audience of 3,500. See Tony's hypnotic presentation like you have never seen it before. VHS 70 minutes

Price: $29.95

Special offers:

Sets I & II: $129.95
Sets I, II, & III: $189.95
Sets I, II, & III and video: $199.95

Please see previous pages for detailed product descriptions.

Order Form

SET I - Personal Development

☐ Self-hypnosis I	$15
☐ Self-hypnosis II	$15
☐ Stop Smoking	$15
☐ Weight Control	$15
☐ Motivation	$15
☐ Deep Relaxation	$15
☐ Complete set	$79.95

SET II - Business Development

☐ Attitude	$15
☐ Creativity	$15
☐ Managing Your Time	$15
☐ Success	$15
☐ Nonverbal Communication	$15
☐ Indirect Suggestion	$15
☐ Complete set	$79.95

SET III - Tony Galie Live

☐ Presentations from around the country $79.95

Video Tape

☐ Tony's hypnotic presentation on video! $29.95

Special packages:

☐ Sets I & II:	$129.95
☐ Sets I, II, & III:	$189.95
☐ Sets I, II, & III and video:	$199.95

Florida residents: please add 6% sales tax.

Ship to: Name _____

Address _____

City _____

State/Zip _____

Phone _____

Fax _____

Total amount due: $ _____

☐ Check enclosed (payable to Anthony Galie Seminars, Inc.)

☐ Bill my: ☐ Visa ☐ MasterCard ☐ AmEx ☐ Discover

Card # _____ Exp. _____

Signature _____

Date _____

Anthony Galie Seminars
2145 North Highway A1A • Indialantic, FL 32903
(800) 462-5748 • (321) 777-1718 • fax (321) 777-8995
e-mail: goals4u@msn.com

Order Form

SET I – Personal Development

- ☐ Self-hypnosis I $15
- ☐ Self-hypnosis II $15
- ☐ Stop Smoking $15
- ☐ Weight Control $15
- ☐ Motivation $15
- ☐ Deep Relaxation $15
- ☐ Complete set $79.95

SET II – Business Development

- ☐ Attitude $15
- ☐ Creativity $15
- ☐ Managing Your Time $15
- ☐ Success $15
- ☐ Nonverbal Communication $15
- ☐ Indirect Suggestion $15
- ☐ Complete set $79.95

SET III – Tony Galie Live

- ☐ Presentations from around the country $79.95

Video Tape

- ☐ Tony's hypnotic presentation on video! $29.95

Special packages:

- ☐ Sets I & II: $129.95
- ☐ Sets I, II, & III: $189.95
- ☐ Sets I, II, & III and video: $199.95

Florida residents: please add 6% sales tax.

Ship to: Name _____

Address _____

City _____

State/Zip _____

Phone _____

Fax _____

Total amount due: $ _____

☐ Check enclosed (payable to Anthony Galie Seminars, Inc.)

☐ Bill my: ☐ Visa ☐ MasterCard ☐ AmEx ☐ Discover

Card # _____ Exp. _____

Signature _____

Date _____

Anthony Galie Seminars
2145 North Highway A1A • Indialantic, FL 32903
(800) 462-5748 • (321) 777-1718 • fax (321) 777-8995
e-mail: goals4u@msn.com